PARTNERS IN THE BETWEEN TIME

Creating Sponsorship Capacity

MARY KATHRYN GRANT, PhD
PATRICIA VANDENBERG, CSC

PUBLISHED BY MINISTRY DEVELOPMENT RESOURCES
MICHIGAN CITY, INDIANA
2004

ISBN 0-9752841-0-X

Printing   5 4 3 2 1

Book design by Celine A. Quinio

CONTENTS

A Word About Words

Careful and precise definitions for sponsorship do not exist. Nor does sponsorship, as it is used in relationship to institutional ministries, have a foundation in canon or civil law—although it has come to carry with it both civil and canonical responsibilities. The word sponsorship was coined in the 1970s and subsequently came into popular usage as a way to describe the relationship between the sponsor, generally a religious congregation, and its institutional works.

The post-Vatican II decade of 1970s was a time of tremendous societal upheaval, a time when many institutions and practices were called into question. It would not be overstating the situation to say that anti-institutionalism was often the prevailing sentiment within religious congregations. The post-Vatican Church saw much greater involvement of the laity in all aspects of church life. At the same time, the 70s saw congregational members begin to question the value of "big corporate" ministries and many individual members elect to serve in non-institutional settings rather than in established institutional ministries. These latter changes gave rise to questions about the very ability of congregations to maintain their schools and hospitals. Often heard in Chapters and Assemblies during this time was the question: "Can it be a (Franciscan, Mercy, Dominican...) facility without any members of the sponsoring congregation serving there?"

The first recorded use of the concept of sponsorship is in 1968 by John McGrath in his discussion of canonical ownership and receipt of public funds. It was not until later, however, that the term came into popular usage. One of the earliest published and workable definitions for sponsorship of Church ministries appeared in a letter of Sister Concilia Moran, RSM, then president of the Sisters of Mercy of the Union. She described sponsorship as: "support of, influence on, and responsibility for a project, program, or institution which furthers the goals of the sponsorship group, the Sisters of Mercy. Sponsorship further implies that the sponsoring group is publicly identified with the project, program or institution and makes certain resources available to them."

This basic description became the foundation for further refinement and focusing of the concept over the

2   *Partners in the Between Time*

intervening years. As recently as 2001, the Catholic Health Association (CHA) of the United States proposed a definition and a set of constitutive elements for its membership which have recently received widespread acceptance.

The CHA has defined *sponsorship* as the relationship within the Catholic Church which allows a juridic person to carry on the healing mission of Jesus. Sponsorship of an incorporated apostolic work consists of the following core elements which involve both canonical and civil realities:

- FIDELITY—faithfulness to the healing mission of Jesus, to the spirit and teachings of the Gospel, and to the teachings of the Church.
- COMMUNITY—a communion of persons committed to a common mission and ministry.
- INTEGRITY—demonstrated integration of mission and core values by all persons as well as in all aspects and activities of the organization.
- STEWARDSHIP—respect for, protection, enhancement and sharing of all the resources used in the ministry.

Several words within the definition and core elements deserve note. The first is the reference to the concept of relationships, which has multiple applications. Most of the parties reacting to the definition as it was being reviewed stressed the importance of this word in describing sponsorship, highlighting the interaction between the sponsor, the juridic person, and the Church of which the ministry is an essential component. It also connotes the relationship between the sponsor and the sponsored works. Additionally, one should note that the connection of sponsorship to the Church and ultimately to Catholic identity is likewise implied in the definition. This connection will be examined later in this volume.

As various canonists assist in the further clarification of the role and responsibility inherent in sponsorship, there may be other nuances identified and promoted over time. Until then, the CHA definition is a good, foundational grounding and has applicability to education as well as healthcare. It must be noted, however, that there are those who prefer the word stewardship to sponsorship and others who struggle to find yet another word to capture the meaning of sponsorship.

For the purposes of this book, *canonical sponsor* refers to the party who is responsible in the eyes of the Church for the works. Most commonly the canonical sponsor is a public juridic person—traditionally a religious congregation or institute or diocese. Public juridic person is a concept in Church law roughly equivalent to a civil corporation and is responsible for the ministry itself, the protection of the assets used in the ministry, and compliance with the laws and teachings of the Church.

In the United States, popular usage has frequently applied the word sponsor to those persons serving as representatives, agents, or trustees of the canonical sponsor. The CHA endeavored to introduce language to clarify this usage, testing such words as sponsor representative or sponsor agent. However, there was general reluctance to introduce these words, hence, the distinction between the canonical sponsor and those sponsoring and referred to as sponsors has blurred.

Additionally, because the structures and models of sponsorship continue to evolve, the term *sponsoring*, rather than *sponsorship*, seems best to capture the living reality. Both terms will be used throughout; however, *sponsorship* will generally refer to the formal, canonical responsibility, and *sponsoring* refers to the evolving application and model development.

One final note. Although *sponsorship* has no canonical roots as noted above, the Vatican in its formal documents has recently used the term. In the Apostolic Exhortation, *Ecclesia in Oceania,* John Paul II actually uses the term in acknowledging the services offered as part of the region's healthcare ministry. He writes, "the Synod Fathers urged support for those who own or sponsor facilities which bring the compassion of Christ to those who suffer..." (34). This may well be the first official usage of the word "sponsor."

In a recent article in *Health Progress*, Sister Sharon Holland, IHM, office head of the Congregation of Institutes for Consecrated Life and Societies of Apostolic Life, describes how English words work their way into the Italian language. She noted that at a meeting in Rome, a speaker, wanting for words, coined *"sponsorizzare"* thereby creating "to sponsor" in Italian. The article itself is an excellent overview of sponsorship from the eyes of the Vatican congregation which handles most American transactions.

The concept of sponsorship, embracing as it does a sacred trust for vital works of mercy, also carries with it notions of spirituality, communion, and discernment which will be explored later in this volume. Two final issues on sponsorship deserve attention here. As the question of the competency and spirituality of the next generation arises, the perennial question is raised: *Is there a distinct lay spirituality or is there only Gospel spirituality, expressed in various life styles and life choices?* What would be the roots of a lay spirituality if not the Gospel? How might a lay spirituality be different? Are not the Gospels the basis of any apostolic spirituality, lived by lay or religious? The position taken in this volume is that there is one spirituality found in the Gospels and acted upon by women and men, religious, lay, cleric; married, single…there is one Lord…

Additionally, sponsorship tends to use Church language which is about apostolates, discernment, patrimony. The majority of lay partners, on the other hand, use business language which is about value-added, asset management, critical success factors, core competencies. Recognizing that readers will be oriented to one or the other of the languages, this volume will attempt to be bilingual. Naturally, the first part of the book dealing with sponsorship will tend to use more Church idiom and the latter parts, dealing with tools, will be more intentionally bilingual. "Nothing is profane," as Teilhard wrote, "for those who know how to see."

PART I

SPONSORSHIP IN THE BETWEEN TIME

"One day Mr. and Mrs. Brown will be
the sponsors of these works....
we must hope and pray
that they will love them as we do."
—Michael Putney, Bishop of Townsville, Queenland, Australia,
Conference on Sponsorship, February 2002

Sponsorship is a complex and multi-faceted reality. To fully grasp the depth of its meaning and importance, it must be examined from many different perspectives. Sponsorship benefits from consideration from at least seven vantage points:

- ANTHROPOLOGICAL—appreciating the variety of roles one may serve in addressing and / or serving during the evolution.

- CANONICAL—grasping the requirements from the standpoint of the Church's expectations, canon law, Church teachings.
- ECCLESIAL—exploring the communal nature of the role and responsibility.
- HISTORICAL—placing the existing model where it is located in terms of the evolving models of sponsorship.
- MINISTERIAL—seeing sponsorship as a unique calling within ministries of the Church.
- SACRAMENTAL—appreciating its role as witness to the mystery of God's loving action in the world.
- THEOLOGICAL—situating the roots of sponsorship in the Gospels with mediation through the tradition and its meaning in contemporary society.

BETWEEN

At a recent gathering in Australia of the leadership of a sponsoring congregation consisting of trustees, executives, and bishops, a discussion about the need to move the current sponsorship model into a new model with significant lay membership evoked a wide range of responses. It occasioned reflection on the meaning of the changes proposed and on the experience of being "in the middle of a major change." In other words, between two quite different models of sponsorship with all that the movement encompasses.

One of those present, Michael Putney, bishop of Townsville, Queensland, Australia, offered some personal musings on the changes under discussion. He commented on how much he cared for and about the apostolic works of his diocese—a hospital, many schools, and outreach social services. This affection translated into his "praying daily for their success and viability" and to "lying awake at night when any one of them is in distress." Thinking ahead to the new model, he said, "One day these ministries will be the responsibility of Mr. and Mrs. Brown. We must hope and pray that they will love them as we do today." These poignant words summed up the hopes (and the fears) inherent in the paradigm shift to lay sponsorship.

One day Mr. and Mrs. Brown may well be exercising canonical responsibilities as sponsors of the ministries giving rise to the question: will they love them as we do?

How well they will care for, lie awake at night for, pray for the ministries over which they have been called to exercise sponsorship depends largely on what happens in this between time. The contemplated change involves many players. With the Church herself as a party to the change, there are three other players: the present sponsor and those currently exercising sponsorship responsibility, the next generation of sponsors, and the apostolic works themselves. It will be critical to take into consideration all four parties and the impact of any changes on them when reflecting on this time between.

Between is a state of being neither here nor there. Between times can be painful and disconcerting; they can create a sense of dislocation and disidentification—a sense of limbo. Waiting to arrive somewhere or waiting for something to come to pass can be a long and painful experience; the time can seem endless and excruciatingly so. Ambiguity, uncertainty, self-questioning, self-doubt may accompany experiences of between times.

Religious congregation-sponsored works are currently experiencing a period of between time. The old models appear no longer viable and the new models are only indefinitely taking shape. The model which most persons involved in the sponsored works are most familiar with will soon become a thing of the past. What is taking its place is still evolving. This is truly a between time.

Paradigm shift

This between time is also commonly known as a "paradigm shift." The concept of paradigm, introduced by Thomas Kuhn in 1962, lends itself to application in any number of arenas. As Kuhn described it, a paradigm shift has five phases:

- the initial, stable period;
- the disquieting appearance of elements which do not fit the existing paradigm;
- a period of destabilization or crisis;
- a transition time; and finally,
- the initial appearance of a new paradigm.

During the middle phases, there is no clarity about the new paradigm. The only experience is that of change. During this particular between time, the paradigm of religiously-sponsored institutional ministries has been changing to a lay-religious partnership model and most likely will ultimately evolve into an entirely lay-sponsored model. But what will sponsorship look like when the paradigm shift has been completed? Who will the new sponsors be? Who will the Mr. and Mrs. Browns be?

Unlike strategic planning where one starts with a clear vision of the end in mind and then creates the strategies and steps to get there, in a paradigm shift one does not see or know the endpoint. It is all middle, all between time. Strategic planning is most successful when the desired goal, objective, or outcome is seen with blazing clarity. In a shifting paradigm, only the past is known with clarity—the future remains an unknown. One is only aware of the shift itself.

The paradigm that is shifting today is that of sponsoring. In order to fully appreciate the magnitude of the changes underway, it may be helpful to review the evolution of sponsorship models. This will also serve as a framework for the subsequent discussion of sponsorship effectiveness. Four phases or waves of sponsorship have been identified, starting with the family business model or the "mom and pop" shop. In this model, all significant roles, decisions, authority, and control were in the hands of the family, the religious congregations that sponsored the organizations. As fewer and fewer congregations were involved in the ministry, the model came to resemble more a franchise in which the family set the standards, established the norms, and held the organizations accountable in its name. The third phase, continuing to employ a business framework, resembles a partnership, characterized by mutuality and interdependence between religious and lay persons. The fourth phase will come into existence when lay sponsorship becomes the prevailing model.

The traditional model, the family business or "mom and pop" shop era, has basically disappeared; the franchise model where the family sets the mission, vision, quality standards, and other expectations is waning as the family members age and dwindle in numbers in active roles in the ministry. The emerging partnership model, wherein religious and their lay counterparts act as partners creating a future together, remains uncharted territory for most. With the establishment of several newer models of public juridic persons, particularly in healthcare, there are examples to study and evaluate as they mature. And beyond that, the endpoint is not clear as a variety of forms begin to emerge.

Figure 1 shows the major facets of the evolution or adaptation drawing from the family business model. It is important to note that in an evolution, change may be gradual and characteristics of a previous stage in the evolution may be found in later stages. There is no clear demarcation between phases in the evolutionary model. For example, it is not uncommon for members of the family, the sponsoring congregation, to expect to receive critical information in advance of others or to be allowed access to buildings and grounds which would not be permitted to non-family members, or other such perks as may have been appropriate when a true family business model was operative.

Figure 1. FOUR WAVES OF SPONSORSHIP

	FAMILY	FRANCHISE	PARTNERSHIP	LAY SPONSORS
Mission	Mission Assurance assumed through numbers	Mission Assurance through standards	Mission Integration demonstrated by assessment efforts	Mission Integration and Accountability prime area of responsibility
Culture	Family traditions and culture prevail	Family culture preserved through "franchise" methods	New culture and tradition being shaped in spirit of mutuality	New culture rooted in tradition and legacy and reshaped for new model
Control	Family control: total	Family control: beginnings of interdependence	Family control: shared; partners incorporated into major roles	Control in hands of new sponsors
Formation	Charism focused/ novitiate	Formation: to family expectations	Formation: into community of persons	Formation: rooted in articulated competencies

REFLECTIONS ON CHANGE

This evolution in sponsoring involves significant change. Change is usually difficult; it threatens one's sense of self-identity and self-security. It calls into question previously held beliefs and assumptions, sometimes without a hint of the beliefs and assumptions that will be their successors. Change often involves unfamiliar and uncomfortable elements. With the changes occurring with sponsorship evolution, relationships are changed, particularly the relationship between members of the sponsoring congregation and lay partners. This evolution involves a changed relationship as well between the new generation of sponsors and the Church and between them and the sponsored works. All four parties are affected.

Institutional ministries, education and healthcare, have had different historical experiences of partnerships with religious and lay persons. Unlike elementary and secondary education, Catholic higher education and healthcare have, from their earliest beginnings, been ministries in which lay and religious have collaborated in the delivery of services and sometime later in the management of facilities. Religious together with lay persons staffed the earliest colleges and hospitals in the United States, with the laity eventually entering the ranks of governance, administration, and management. On the other hand, initially, religious women and men for the most part staffed Catholic schools. It has been noted that only a generation ago, only one-third of all teachers in Catholic schools were lay, while today that number is over 90 percent. What preparation will help assure a smooth transition in the future? To some extent, it will be acknowl-

Partners in the Between Time

edging the continued need for lay leadership and making provisions for development, formation, and incorporation.

In recent times, given the impetus of Vatican II, formal leadership formation efforts by congregational sponsors, and the increased commitment and involvement of the laity, helped assure a continuity of mission and values. Vital to this approach was a spirit of accountability; then as responsibilities of the laity increased and moved in the direction of increasing participation in governance, the change was less disruptive. More recently, with the decline in the number of religious women and men available to serve in governance roles and increasingly in sponsorship roles as well, the obligation to develop sponsorship capacity and to prepare for an orderly transition to lay sponsorship has become an imperative. Orchestrating that transition while the congregations are still vitally involved in the ministry and have a clear vision and plan for how to proceed is a task that congregations and their lay partners began more than a decade ago.

When the family business was the prevalent model, it was believed that the family members charged with sponsorship understood and embraced their responsibilities. In many instances, this was far from the case. More often than not, individuals elected to congregational leadership assumed the responsibilities of sponsorship as a necessary part of their duties, primary of which was spiritual leadership of the congregation. Sponsorship was a component of the duties ascribed to leadership roles and rarely a factor in choosing congregational leadership.

Many congregational leaders will admit that they had not given sponsorship much thought, if any, throughout the discernment and election processes. They speak more of "falling into" the role of sponsor as result of being called or elected to serve in leadership role. Few would be able to say that they actually responded intentionally to a call to serve as in a sponsoring role or saw it as an essential responsibility within the duties of congregational leadership.

This is all changing. Congregations faced with fewer, older members have long realized that the growing complexity of the ministries require expertise and experience beyond what its members might have or that they might need to expand or complement that expertise. Vatican II catalyzed ministries to involve lay persons in increasingly more significant roles in management and governance. The duties of sponsor, however, until recently, have remained the domain of the congregation's leadership and were often invisible even to its own membership—much less to lay persons involved in various capacities in the ministry. Clearly, governing boards respected and appreciated *reserved powers*, the traditional locus of sponsorship responsibilities, but the full range of responsibilities and duties of sponsorship were largely invisible.

Sponsorship Responsibilities

What are those duties and responsibilities known as sponsorship? Canon law gives guidance by way of two broad areas: the faithful administration or oversight of the ministry and the preservation or protection of assets used in the ministry, the *ecclesiastical goods* (the physical assets, property and buildings). It is the faithful administration of the ministry, ultimately, which most inspires and animates sponsorship as a ministry. This is not to negate the need and duty of protecting Church property as a means to insure the future viability and vitality of the ministry, but only to say that the motivation and intrinsic reward for serving in the role of sponsor, as well as the sense of sacred responsibility, emanates from the faithful governance and oversight of the ministry itself.

Looking at these two major areas of responsibility, it is easy to see how reserved powers were embraced as the concrete manifestation of the fiduciary responsibility of the sponsoring group. Membership corporations, with their two tiers of authority, clearly segmented the responsibilities between sponsorship exercised through reserved powers and the remaining areas of governance delegated to the governing board.

A measure of the understanding of the fiduciary responsibilities of the sponsor may be found in a progression of questions. Who has not cringed to hear the question: "What do the Sisters want?" suggesting little internalization of the decision-making. When the question evolves to "What would the Sisters do?" there is deeper personal appropriation of the discernment process. The final query,

Figure 2. THE EVOLVING QUESTION	
Early phase	What do the Sisters want?
Middle phase	What would the Sisters do?
Mature phase	What should we do?

"What should we do?" reflects the most mature and internalized position, and embodies a spirit of community.

The exploration of the this final question points to the theological dimensions of sponsorship and underscores the imperative for organizational as well as individual competency in discernment. But, first it will be necessary to examine the concept of sponsorship effectiveness.

Sponsorship effectiveness

Having examined briefly the duties of sponsorship, the next step in this transition to newer models is to identify those personal and institutional competencies which would assure sponsorship effectiveness. Full exploration of the dynamics of faithful sponsorship, or sponsorship effectiveness, is an evolving effort in most instances. The concept of sponsorship effectiveness has two dimensions: institutional and individual. How is sponsorship organizationally exercised and how faithfully is this exercised? What are the characteristics of institutional or organizational fidelity? Secondly, how effective are those serving in sponsorship roles? What competencies do they exhibit? Answering these questions is the first step toward setting in place tools for assessing and developing sponsorship capacity.

Several components of sponsorship effectiveness suggest themselves. These are:
- fulfillment of the mission of the organization which is animated by the Gospel and informed by the charism and culture of the founding congregation(s);

- stewardship of the tangible and intangible resources of the ministry: its people, its finances, its heritage, its assets, its patrimony, and
- recognition that the works themselves are essential ministries of the Church.

These three essential components of sponsorship effectiveness require certain competencies among those serving as sponsors. Principal among these competencies are skills in theological reflection or discernment and in creating and nurturing a spirit of communion among those involved. Exploring the way to identify the next generation of sponsors gives rise to the question: Is sponsorship a unique calling in today's Church? Should sponsorship be viewed differently from other organizational roles? Is it so substantively different from management and governance that it should be seen differently?

THE CALLING OF "SPONSORS"

As St. Paul writes, there are many gifts, many parts and pieces in the mosaic called Church. Given the tremendous responsibility involved in serving in a role of sponsor, one might argue that it is timely to name this a unique service, a ministry itself or perhaps a special calling within the Church. The call to service comes with baptism and is incumbent on all Christians. How that call is exercised is a matter of personal and communal discernment.

Vatican II opened the doors to greater lay participation in the ministries of the Church and the response was multi-faceted. There followed significantly greater lay involvement in parish councils, administrative and governance roles in education and healthcare; catechetic and chaplaincy roles opened up to laity. Seminaries opened their doors to women and men who desired deeper theological education; pastoral associate positions were created and filled by both religious and lay men and women. It would only be a matter of time before participation in sponsorship roles would be on the horizon.

Service as sponsor is a unique role in the Church. Basically it involves being responsible to the Church for a ministry of the Church. It means preserving, protecting, ensuring the integrity as well as the future viability of those organizations established for carrying out the works of mercy. It means caring about them even to the point of "lying awake at night when they are in distress." Accepting the responsibility to serve in a sponsoring role means being willing to engage in discernment, dialogue, and theological reflection and to strive to create a community of committed persons with the others serving in the role of sponsor. Thus starts the creation of a range of competencies for those called to exercise this role.

Sponsorship is truly a uniquely new role for lay women and men. In this between time, the current sponsors and their potential successors have many important tasks. It has been proposed that the current sponsors could serve in the role of mentors, teachers, guides for the new sponsors. A richer and perhaps more rewarding way of viewing the interaction between the present and future sponsors is that of accompaniment, of journeying with, companioning, in which the road is traveled together. Accompaniment is conditioned on the concepts of mutuality, interdependence, and co-creation linked with the belief that human beings are created for social life in community. Pursuing this thinking leads immediately to an exploration of the theological and communitarian roots of sponsorship.

It is a common practice among religious congregations to debate control vs. influence. Fearful of what might happen when there are no members to oversee the established ministries, some congregations argued that control was an absolute necessity while others adopted influence as their mode of interacting and governing. Another way of reframing this question is to talk about control vs. collaboration or co-creation. If one understands co-creation to embrace the concepts of theological reflection within a community of persons committed to the mission of the ministry, then the need for control in the absolute sense diminishes. The rest of this volume endorses co-creation in community.

THEOLOGICAL AND COMMUNITARIAN DIMENSIONS OF SPONSORSHIP

For years, there has been a call for a theology of sponsorship and sponsoring. The call for the latter has been tentatively answered in recognizing the call to ministry and to service grounded in baptism. All Christians are called to service and to communion/community. One may even go so far as to name sponsoring as a special vocation or calling in the Church when this is a primary focus of one's life or work. It is no small task to be called to be responsible for those organizations that serve as a means of performing the works of mercy; to assure their relevancy to community needs, to insure the viability and vitality in the future; and to do so in a community of persons equally and passionately committed to the same end. Additionally, holding each other accountable for the quality and integrity of the mission, of decisions made, of contracts signed, of curriculum standards, and of services offered are in the spirit of community.

Where does that leave the search for the theology of sponsorship itself? Perhaps that is the wrong question; perhaps the question would be better phrased as the theological dimensions of sponsorship. What theological images anchor the understanding of sponsorship and sponsoring?

Three images in the New Testament suggest themselves as possible foundational influences: the concept of servant-leader as portrayed by the washing of the feet; the notion of scarce-yet-abundant resources in the multiplication of the loaves; and the expansiveness and rootedness of the vine and the branches. Other images may also serve yet somehow these three, alone and together, capture something of the essence of sponsorship today: service, capacity, and rootedness.

Grounded in the self-sacrifice of servant-leadership imaged in the washing of feet, women and men religious, and later their lay colleagues, humbly accepted appointments to govern and to be responsible as sponsors of the magnificent and creative organizations established for education and healthcare ministries. The image has profound implications in establishing the criteria by which to identify trustees and call sponsors to this form of ministry and is an invitation to examine more deeply the role of servant-leader.

The second image, the multiplication of the loaves, speaks directly to the current state of sponsorship. Today a sense of diminishment might be the prevailing sentiment, of not having sufficient resources for the needs of the day, but that is only to be overturned by an experience of abundance as bread is broken and shared with more than enough for the moment. Opening the role of sponsorship to include others called to serve in this capacity—providing, nurturing, and sustenance, as it were—offering whatever one has for the good of the whole, what more powerful image of the call to sponsorship today could one suggest.

Lastly, the image of the vine and the branches, often used in other applications, speaks to both rootedness and to expansion and growth. Under the right conditions, the healthy vine yields many branches and good fruit. Rooted in the soil of the Gospel and nurtured by the culture and charism of the original sponsoring congregation, the vine can thrive.

SPONSORSHIP: A SACRAMENTAL PERSPECTIVE

What is the role of today's sponsor in relation to the works themselves? To the next generation of sponsors? One might look to two sources for an answer. To the sacramental practice of having a sponsor and to a theology of accompaniment. The two notions are not dissimilar. In the Catholic Church one has a sponsor in two sacraments: baptism and confirmation. The sponsor's role in these sacraments is to mentor, nurture, guide, encourage. These, it would seem, are adaptable to the sponsors' role with regard to preparing the next generation of sponsors for institutional ministry.

A theology of sponsorship must of its very nature be grounded and rooted in a spirit of community/communion. In many circles today, the word community has negative connotations. For some it congers up "touchy-feely" memories from the 1960-70s; for others it brings to mind memories of not so happy experiences of religious community life. For yet others it is a painful reminder of the failure of the post-Vatican II era to create parish communities which are welcoming and supportive. Putting all these negative connotations aside, the spirit of *communio* or the creation of a community of committed persons remains a vital underpinning of authentic sponsorship.

Any theology of sponsorship will need to address the challenges, the direction, and the radical reshaping of its response to the times. It will also need to be created in a spirit of *praxis*, action informed by theological reflection, a mutual examination of the times, reflection on the tradition, and a spirituality of discernment. It must affirm education or healthcare as a vital ministry of the Church.

If one accepts the four attributes of sponsorship as identified by CHA—fidelity, stewardship, integrity, and community/communion—one can easily see the interdependency of the four attributes. Discernment of fidelity is grounded in and reinforces the integrity of the organization; discernment requires community, unity of mind and heart in pursuit of the common mission, the common good. Stewardship is incumbent on the sponsors out of a profound respect for the past and in anticipation of a vital future.

24

James and Evelyn Whitehead thoughtfully explore the concept of stewardship in *The Promise of Partnership*. Focusing on the parable of the good steward, the authors identify three qualities of a faithful steward: a servant, not an owner, demonstrates seasoned reliability, and acts in the absence of the owner. The steward is "deprived of independence and possessiveness...responsible for what [we] do not own." In this "paradox of non-possessive care," the community of stewards is described as a ministry group with shared values, committed to a common action and acting out of a common concern.

Sponsorship, too, involves a ministry group, the persons accepting responsibility as sponsors over a ministry of the Church which they do not own. They are bound together in community by common, shared values. They hold in trust a ministry organized for the works of mercy and to meet and serve the needs of a particular locale, in other words, to fulfill its mission.

Sponsors endeavor to be of one heart and mind in acting with fidelity and integrity to make decisions congruent with the mission, to select leadership imbued with the values and alive with the mission, and to assure the assets, tangible and intangible, are not only preserved but enhanced in order to ensure its future. These goals are best achieved by a community of persons united by a passion for the good of those being served, laying aside self-interest, striving for the common good, and enabling and holding one another accountable for the sacred trust conveyed by being called sponsor.

Sponsorship is an invitation to co-create a future even greater than the past. It is a call to challenge and to celebrate, to support and sustain, to insure the decisions and actions of the organization and its members are truly the public face of its mission. It requires integrity within the organization, in its services and in its people.

There are two dimensions to the question how to prepare for the future. First is the identification of the next generation of sponsors—who are they and how to prepare them for this role—and second is how to prepare for them.

The issue of how to prepare the next generation of sponsors has of late begun to receive a lot of attention. Concepts such as mentoring and coaching, borrowed from contemporary management practices, are becoming popular yet seem to be wanting. Mentoring connotes something more episodic, periodic touching base, receiving counsel, asking questions. Accompaniment carries with it a more interpersonal dimension, being with, walking along together, seeking, discerning, and reflecting together.

The adaptation or evolution of sponsorship models changes many relationships both within the congregations that had historically sponsored the organizations and between the current and successor sponsors. These between times demand careful attention to how these relationships are affected by the changes. One congregation found it extremely helpful to very openly discuss the pending changes and their impact on existing relationships, as many of the players would remain the same only in changed roles. All agreed that there needed to be great clarity about who was responsible for what. They also recognized that to assure a smooth transition, not only accountability, but also communication and relationship building needed tending.

A weekend retreat with all concerned parties identified how both the formal accountabilities and communications would be handled. That was the easy part. With the aid of a facilitator they also discussed the need for both formal and informal communications and special efforts at maintaining existing good relationships with changed roles. All agreed that there might be conflicting expectations, as the same individuals would be relating to one another in new roles. Three issues emerge: accountability, communication, and relationships.

For example, some of the issues of accountability under the new structure might naturally overlap or be confused with items for communication. To clarify further, it proved helpful to role-play a few pending items, to situate them as items/issues of accountability; items/ issues for communication only and not accountability, and items/issues shared to foster and nurture either existing or new relationships. Identifying what fell into each category helped, noting overlapping items as well as naming expectations, particularly in the area of communications. Everyone also agreed to recognize there might be missteps and even some painful moment s when expectations would need to be adjusted to the new reality. The clarification of accountability, communication, and relationship went a long way toward easing the transition.

Preparing for any adaptation or change in sponsorship involves two phases: preparing the next generation of sponsors and knowing when this transition in roles has been successful. The first task, preparing those individuals who will be invited to serve in sponsoring roles, has several components: identifying the competencies each sponsor must possess, screening for these competencies and for a fit with the mission, vision, and culture of the organization; engaging all parties in on-going education and development; incorporating the new sponsors by forming a community of persons committed to the integrity of the organization; and evaluating sponsorship effectiveness.

The latter evaluation process has two prongs: evaluation of the individuals serving in the role and evaluation of sponsorship, itself. To do these two tasks effectively requires the existence of articulated norms or standards of performance and a defined process for the conduct of the evaluation itself. Part II will explore these tasks more fully.

Preparing for the Next Generation of Sponsors

Being clear about who would constitute the next generation of sponsors and what skills and competencies they must have is only half the task. Preparing *for them* is, in many cases, a more difficult task. The need to evolve sponsorship models is a given. And those responsible for overseeing the transition may face difficult times and difficult-to-deal-with personal responses, often from those closest to them—members of their own congregations and trusted lay colleagues.

Sponsorship evolution is complicated by two factors: the degree to which the self-identity of the congregation itself is tied to its institutions and the numbers of its members who have been or are engaged in ministry where the change or adaptation is contemplated. Congregations engaged in a single ministry such as education or health-care often experience a greater sense of loss and of lost identity than those with diversified ministries. The latter seem to have greater resilience in the face of change.

There is also a correlation between the number of members who have had a relationship to the organization undergoing change—such as having been a student or having taught in the school, having been born or nursed in the hospital—and the impact of the loss. The greater and/or longer the involvement, the more far reaching the experience of change or loss appears to be.

More recently, the trends observed earlier—growing complexity in the ministries themselves, fewer "family" members to serve in any capacity, greater diversification of ministries, and more avenues for direct ministerial service—has led to the creation of newer models of sponsorship and, in some cases, to an eventual withdrawal from sponsorship by the religious congregation. As might be anticipated, changes of this magnitude elicit a myriad of responses both from members of the congregation themselves as well as lay colleagues who have journeyed with them, sometimes for decades. Studying the responses to these changes as they are occurring will be instructive for those who must face the need to change or evolve in the future.

The evolution or adaptation being discussed here represents profound change—changes that may significantly alter the self-identity of the sponsoring congregation if it has so identified with its institutional ministries. A congregation with several schools that have had to be closed over the past

15 years faces an organizational identity crisis which one member has described as "we have gone from a ministry in academy boarding schools, to co-ed college prep schools, to infirmaries for our older members—all within the past 20 years. I am not sure where I see my ministry today."

Navigating changes of this magnitude requires two sets of skills and sensitivities: grief-work and change management. All change, even the most welcomed, involves loss and loss requires grieving. Working through the process of grieving is essential to moving through the inherent changes. Each individual will proceed at his/her own pace, sometimes moving forward, sometimes backward, sometimes not moving at all. It should be remembered that the process itself is not linear; moreover it is cumulative in that prior grief-work, not completed, most likely will be re-experienced in this new series of events perceived as loss. It is by anticipating responses such as are outlined here that all involved may be better prepared to respond more sensitively to someone at any point in the cycle.

There are at least six distinct roles individuals may assume in the midst of these changes: the passionate pioneer, the resigned supporter, the late bloomer, the critical observer, the conscientious objector, and the puzzled and perplexed. These roles were first identified as relating to members of sponsoring congregations, however, they apply equally well to lay partners in the ministry.

THE PASSIONATE PIONEERS

Often leading the charge are the passionate pioneers, those capable of seeing into the future, identifying where the organization needs to be headed, and leading in that

Partners in the Between Time

direction. They are the futurists who, having seen a need for change, begin to lay careful plans and well thought-out strategies for either the changed role of the religious congregation or the necessary evolution of the model of sponsorship. They are visionary and charismatic. They are also misunderstood and often maligned. They must sound the clarion call for change and generally lead the initiative. This pioneer may be the president of the organization, the leadership of the congregation, or the chair of the board.

Their sense of loss is no less keen than that of the others, however, they have often had to do their grief work privately and earlier than the rest. They may appear to be unaffected by the sense of loss as they must inspire hope and confidence in the future and in the capacity of the organization to change. They may feel very much alone and, if there is no widespread support for the movement, they may feel abandoned by others.

THE RESIGNED SUPPORTERS

Behind the passionate pioneers are the resigned supporters. These individuals are logical and analytical, they have recognized and accepted the inevitability of movement but are not its champions. They may be counted on to support the changes as they occur but not to take any leadership or public role in achieving the desired end.

Often they have grieved privately and others do not see them experiencing sorrow or loss. They, too, may be viewed as dispassionate and uncaring when in fact they may care very deeply, but internally, so that no one knows of their pain.

The late bloomers

The late bloomers are generally those who have experienced some ambivalence toward the ministry or who have historically been disengaged from it. They may belong to the group that valued direct service over "corporate ministries," or possibly who previously took an "anti-institutional" stand. Then, as the changes are proposed, they begin to take a more active interest in the corporate ministry. They will often offer to serve, claiming that they "never had been asked," or had a chance to serve before.

They come to the ministry late and feeling somewhat disenfranchised. They may appear quite emotional with their grief work being more in evidence than the previous depictions. Their sense of loss is deep and perhaps marked with regrets. There may be a bit of bartering in their grief work. If they only had a chance to serve, things might be different. Late bloomers may be members of the congregation or newly appointed trustees.

The critical observers

Detail oriented and skeptical, the critical observers will be most vigilant about how the decision is effected. These are the persons who raise the questions of legality, both canonically or civilly. They are vigilant about the details and actions being proposed. In one instance, a "critical observer" engaged her own canon lawyer friend to double-check the steps being taken by her congregation.

Critical observers do not necessarily oppose the direction being taken but are critical of how it is being executed. They may also appear cold and uncaring; more interested in the rightness of the process than the psychological and emotional impact of the decisions themselves.

THE CONSCIENTIOUS OBJECTORS

On the other hand, the conscientious objectors do oppose the change, sometimes they oppose any change. These individuals find change difficult to accept, offering observations such as "It isn't broken, so don't fix it." Or imploring more faith in providence, "We went through harder times than these... and God always saw us through."

Sometimes these objectors will go to any lengths to stop or thwart the endeavor. It may appear that they are in denial, refusing to accept the need to change or adapt. They may also reflect anger that someone is moving with a progressive agenda. These may be persons with long, personal involvement with or relationship to the sponsored works—long time faculty, board members, physicians, for example.

THE PUZZLED AND PERPLEXED

This last category includes those who are recently attracted to the ministry and may have an idealized view of the situation facing the organization. They may be new board members or newer congregational members who cannot see why things might need to change. Indeed, they are "puzzled and perplexed" that the congregation seems to be withdrawing from the ministry at the very time they are becoming involved. They have wholeheartedly embraced the idea of service and ministry and find the rea-

Figure 3. An anthropological look at change			
Role	Description	Personal Attributes	Stage of Grief Work
Passionate pioneer	Futurist: sees need to change	Dynamic, charismatic	Anticipates and works through privately
Resigned supporter	Deems need for change to be inevitable	Logical, analytic	Appears to have anticipated and begun grief work
Late bloomer	Feels passed over and slighted; never given chance to serve	Emotional, spontaneous	Appears to be in stage of bargaining; if he/she had played a role then...
Critical observer	Feels need to assure all I's are dotted and t's crossed	Detail oriented, skeptical	Camouflages grief with concern for rightness of process
Conscientious objector	Feels duty bound to questions and oppose effort	Risk averse, critical	Seems to be in denial; sees no need to change and uses resources to oppose
Puzzled and perplexed	Newer to ministry and confused by actions about to be taken	Thoughtful, searching	Is also in denial; surprised and disappointed at turn of events

sons for the changes difficult to understand and accept. In their new enthusiasm and zeal, they do not yet see the need to grieve. They are often thoughtfully searching for answers as well as for their place in the ministry.

Preparing for change

At a critical time in the history and evolution of institutional ministries and religious life where major changes in both are converging, it is imperative to engage in theological reflection and anthropological observation. Believing the works of mercy to be central to the mission of the Church and working for the future viability and vitality of those structures and roles established for that purpose demands not only a little faith but also a critical imagination to see new ways of realizing the kingdom in our day.

QUESTIONS FOR REFLECTION

• What is your Scriptural image of sponsorship? What does it mean for you? If you had done this exercise 10 years ago, would it have been your image then? Why or why not?

• What are some of the myths about sponsorship that you cling to? Its current effectiveness? Its permanence?

• What are your deepest hopes for the future?

• What are your strongest fears for the future?

• Draw a time line of your relationship to the ministry. What are some of the highlights, times of great achievement? What were some of the times of challenge and stress?

• What does this timeline tell you about this ministry? About your relationship to it?

• What does your sustained faithfulness tell you about the future?

Partners in the Between Time

PART II

TOOLS FOR THE BETWEEN TIME

THE MEANING OF MISSION

"It helps us now and then to step back and take the long view.
The kingdom is always beyond our effort...
No set of goals and objectives includes everything...
We are prophets of a future not our own."
—Archbishop Oscar Romero

The transition to a new and as yet not-experienced form of sponsorship, as described in Part I of this volume, has the potential to create great hope that the legacy, the mission and values, of the original sponsors will endure, on the one hand, and give rise to considerable anxiety and concern about the unknown, on the other hand. Much of the hope can be assured and the concern allayed by a strong, demonstrable commitment to and integration of the mission and values of the organization.

Mission is and should be a dynamic tool for renewing and sustaining the organization during turbulent times, and times of change. The greatest assurance of continuity and fidelity in the evolution or adaptation of the form of sponsorship—from the traditional, congregational model ultimately to lay sponsorship—are the following:

- degree to which the mission of the organization permeates every action,

- visibility in every dimension of its activities,

- witnessed by every employee, faculty member, trustee, associate, physician, volunteer.

The fullness and faithfulness of mission is realized when—

- mission directs all decision-making and strategic planning,

- mission is the basis of hiring, rewarding, promoting, and retaining faculty, staff, employees,

- mission forms the foundation of budgeting and resource allocation,

- "mission-driven" is a core competence of the organization.

Mission should give the organization its critical edge, its anchor in difficult times, its recruiting leverage. Mission is also the ground and source of the organization's culture.

Mission may all-too-often be taken for granted or viewed as merely an inspirational or motivational statement, but it is so much more than that. It is the very ground and purpose of the organization. Evidence of mission fulfillment can be found in the annual audit, the organization's accreditation reports, its student retention rates, its patient and employee satisfaction surveys, its clinical outcomes, its graduation rates. It may also be found in its community service and service learning, its charity care and community benefit efforts, its chaplaincy and campus ministry.

Mission expresses the purpose, the *raison d'etre* of the organization. In an age of rapid redesign, competing at the speed of internet commerce exchange, and unforgiving markets, religiously-sponsored organizations seek to leverage their unique identity in order to achieve both business goals and mission fulfillment. While there are many ways in which non-profit organizations may seek to emulate their for-profit competitors, there is one unique asset non-profits can and should capitalize on—the power a mission-centered organization enjoys in the face of these myriad challenges.

Non-profit organizations possess unique attributes that can serve them well and position them securely for the future during these changing times. These attributes include—

- attracting and retaining, mobilizing and motivating a committed faculty, staff, or workforce;
- allocating scarce resources strategically and appropriately;
- choosing wisely and measuring both business and mission success.

Attention to these matters, to mission fulfillment and integration, are means of assuring the fidelity of the ministry and ultimately are evidences of sponsorship effectiveness.

The concept of *value creation* is popular in management literature today. What greater value creation opportunity is there in the service sector than to be successful at both business and mission fulfillment. This section explores proven ways to achieve optimal success in reaching business objectives at the same time being faithful to the organization's mission and assuring sponsorship effectiveness.

The first part of this section on mission will explore the meaning of mission and mission-centeredness. This will be followed by a detailed discussion of how mission is the platform of organizational architecture, including illustrations of two mission-based core processes—a Mission Assessment and Development Process and a process for using mission in strategic planning sometimes called a Mission Discernment Process. The final section will describe how mission can be infused into two significant other areas—corporate integrity and human resource practices. Three additional topics will be woven into the discussion: an examination of mission's role in informing and shaping the organizational culture, mission and community, and finally a brief look at the creation and evolution of infrastructure supports, the mission committees and mission leadership.

WHAT IS MISSION?

Management literature is replete with arguments that mission statements serve a salutary role in organizations. Authors tout the value of mission statements in aligning the organization's objectives and purposes, in clarifying the organization's purpose and providing a solid ground for value creation. But how are these lofty objectives achieved and measured? How do they become the basis for both organizational and individual assessment and development? How do they assure the organization's fundamental integrity and sponsorship effectiveness?

As early as 1973, Peter Drucker defined mission. "To satisfy the customer is the mission and purpose of every business. The question 'What is our business?' can, therefore, be answered only by looking at the business from the outside, from the point of view of the customer and market."[1] In the years that followed this declaration of the meaning of mission, other critical dimensions have been added. In a later writing, Drucker agrues that unless the mission statement is operational, it will be viewed as "good intentions."[2] Today one would include an emphasis on *stakeholder* interest in mission fulfillment. It is in operationalizing the mission that the organization achieves its purposes and fulfills its accountability to its stakeholders, in this case stakeholders include its sponsors, and ultimately to the Church in whose mission and ministry it participates.

Mission articulates the organization's reason for being. As clear as this may seem, there is some misunderstanding about mission. It is sometimes confused with a statement of beliefs or philosophy, or the organization's vision or role statement. And while it has considerable relationship to and influence on these matters, it is distinct from them.

Organizational beliefs or philosophy are the foundational and more global truths held about people, work, time, and service. They are the grounding of the mission and are sometimes promoted as a statement of the underlying philosophy. Conversely, the organization's vision and its role statement, in particular, are finite and time-bound. They have a horizon and parameters that may change as the mode of service, site, or construct of or demand for services change. Contrasted to the role statement found in the strategic plan, the mission statement presents a clear and identifiable locus of accountability and the source of motivation and pride.

Unlike the philosophy or vision statements, the mission statement is an enduring articulation of the central purpose and social contribution of the organization. Given that, it can be the measure against which all decisions are made; the criteria by which employees are hired, developed, and rewarded. Mission is the grounding of the organization in concrete, accessible terms. It is also a unifying and integrating force within the organization.

To illustrate, following is a mission statement for a faith-based healthcare system:

> *Faithful to the spirit of the Congregation*
> *of the Sisters of the Holy Cross [the sponsors],*
> *Holy Cross Health System exists*
> *to witness Christ's love through excellence*
> *in the delivery of health services,*
> *motivated by respect for those we serve.*
> *We foster a climate that empowers*
> *those who work with us*
> *while stewarding our human and financial resources.*

The essence of this statement is captured by four focal points around which all processes and practices in the organization have been built:

- fidelity to the founding vision;
- excellence in the core business;
- empowerment of those involved in the service delivery; and
- stewardship of scarce and valued resources.

These four central elements ultimately provide the framework for mission integration into human resource practices, performance management and development, institutional mission assessment, and mission discernment when applied to strategic direction setting and planning. Figure 4 gives the highlights of how the four elements were identified, applied, and measured.

As differentiated from role, vision, and philosophy statements, the mission statement of an organization is intended to be enduring and should require changing or updating only infrequently. In fact, the mission statement may require only minor modification, as the times demand. The evolution of Disney's mission statement is an illustration of the modifications required over time. Disney's mission today is: *To create happiness for all people everywhere.* This statement represents only two changes since the original mission was articulated.

The original statement, written at a time when the primary market for Disney products and services was children, called for creating "happiness for children." Several decades later when families had become the primary market, the mission was restated to focus on

Figure 4. Mission Integration: Sample Indicators

	Fidelity	Excellence	Empowerment	Stewardship
Meaning and application	To the mission and values of the organization To the heritage and reputation of the sponsors To the teachings and directives of the church	In performance outcomes: • Student performance; • Clinical outcomes; • Service delivery	Of faculty, students, employees, patients, volunteers, trustees	Of human resources • Low turnover; • Employee development Of financial resources Of environmental resources
Indicators	Periodic mission assessment and subsequent development efforts Mission discernment in decision-making	Accreditation reports Quality indicators Dashboards Satisfaction surveys	Retention rates Graduation rates Diversity agendas Worksite spirituality Compensation and reward systems	Audits Reducing and cycling Environmental awareness Employee turnover

creating "happiness for families." When it was evident that the contemporary idea of family had changed and that people of all ages, relationships, and circumstances were Disney's market, the mission statement was altered to address "people" rather than children or families. Additionally, to embrace explicitly all of Disney's product lines and services, the concept of "everywhere" was added: to "create happiness for all people [all ages and walks of life] everywhere [theme parks, retail stores…]." Clearly, the essence of the mission, to create happiness, had never been changed—only the target market and expanded focus. It would do well for organization's to examine and renew their mission statements only nuancing them as needed.

Figure 5. SAMPLE REVISIONS OF DISNEY'S MISSION STATEMENT

To create happiness for *children*

To create happiness for *families*

To create happiness for *people everywhere*

A word about *whose mission*. During times of change and evolution, clarity and precision of ideas and of language are essential. This is particularly true in relationship to mission and to whose mission—the sponsor's or the organization's? Frequently, there is a temptation to think of the organization as embracing the mission of the congregation and to speak in terms of fulfilling the congregation's, the sponsor's mission, and sometimes even of fulfilling the congregation's charism. This confusion about whose mission will lead to problems down the road and raise issues of self-identity for both the congregation and for the organization.

Each sponsored organization should have its own, unique mission, separate and apart from the congregational mission. This mission may refer to the congregation's mission and values and it should emanate from them, but must have its own statement of mission. Within a multi-unit system and in an effort to promote a common culture, there may be a single mission statement for the system and individual role statements for each member organization. Clarity about whose mission is essential to help insure a smooth transition and to be clear about what is actually involved in organizational changes and transitions. Further, differentiating the organization's mission from that of the congregation's clearly posits responsibility for mission fulfillment at the door, so to speak, of the organization itself.

Additionally, the mission statement should be equally explicable and meaningful to all constituents—to members of the faculty, to the security guard, and the surgeon. It should be applicable to decision-making at the bedside, the blackboard, and the board room. It should provide the criteria for strategy and direction. In other words, every aspect of organizational life should reflect the mission and values of the entity.

Stephen Shortell describes this phenomenon as "holographic," with the part containing the whole as in a holograph. The mission should be the archetypal holograph, embedded discernibly in every expression of the operation; it is its DNA as it were. Clearly, the mission statement is a principle of organizational alignment. In Figure 4 which details examples of fidelity, excellence, empowerment, and stewardship, some of the overlap or holographic nature of mission integration is evident. For example, satisfaction surveys flow from respect for the dignity of the person, relate to excellence and empowerment, and lead to stewardship of human resources.

It goes without saying that when an organization deviates from its mission and values, the response to and regard for the mission may be cynical and sour. When faculty, staff, and others have embraced the mission and all that it stands for, they are justifiably disappointed and dismayed when the organization or its leadership is not perceived to be faithful to who it says it is. Therefore, periodic reflection on and assessment of the strength of mission integration is an essential act of the organization.

It is important to note that there is little empirical research on the value of mission statements in relation to performance, except in the area of healthcare with the following published works by Christopher K. Bart: "Mission Statement Rationales and Organizational Alignment in Not-for-Profit Healthcare Sector," *Healthcare Management Review*, Fall 1998 and "Mission Statements in Canadian Not-for-Profit Hospitals: Does the Process Matter?", *Healthcare Management Review,* Spring 2000. These studies demonstrate the relationship between a hospital's mission statement and its performance and the importance of the processes of mission creation and implementation. There is a great need for more empirical research on the role mission plays in organizational alignment, performance, and outcomes of education and healthcare institutions.

In short, the mission statement should explicitly state why the organization exists; how competing interests will be reconciled; how resources will be allocated; how time and money will be spent. The mission statement should also motivate the workforce and associates to strive for excellence in both service and outcomes. It is essentially the organization's moral compass and by so being, it becomes that of the individuals—employees, faculty, staff, administration, associates as well.

Unfortunately, mission is sometimes reduced to employee "feel good" endeavors. One frequently hears the cliché, "No margin, no mission," in a way that dichotomizes the organization's mission and its business purposes and sets one against the other as if they were competing realities. The very achievement of a margin should be integral to mission achievement, as should quality outcomes; student, faculty, employee retention, customer satisfaction; and market preservation, growth, or diversification. There should be no aspect of the "business" of an organization that is not shaped and informed by the mission and which in turn contribute to the fulfillment of the mission.

The relationship between mission and other aspects of the organization, particularly alignment within the organization with the mission, is explored in a theoretical framework in a significant study by Robert W. Terry. Terry creates a framework that can be simplified by examining four components: mission, power, structure, and resources.[3] Mission is the statement that defines the organization. Power refers to the distribution of authority and responsibility to carry out the mission; structure includes those sys-

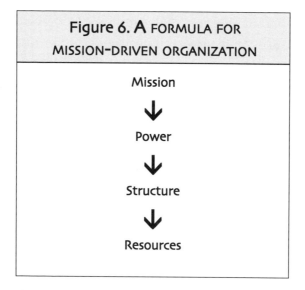

Figure 6. A FORMULA FOR MISSION-DRIVEN ORGANIZATION

Mission

⬇

Power

⬇

Structure

⬇

Resources

tems, policies, and practices at the disposal of the mission; and resources are the tangible means of fulfilling the mission, the equipment, dollars, personnel, buildings, etc.

Terry's complete framework includes three other pieces (existence, meaning, and fulfillment), however, the abbreviated framework is highly effective in identifying the extent to which mission is the starting point and organizing principle for planning and decision-making, resource allocation, and organizational alignment. This framework sets the stage for examining the core process of mission assessment and development.

In Terry's model, mission is the central driver and each of the other components flows from and supports the mission. Terry provides a powerful framework for grasping and explicating the centrality of mission. He observes that organizations often seek to solve matters at a level below the problem. Moreover, he argues that organizations, departments, units seek additional resources when structure is often the issue; they reorganize and restructure when power is what needs to be addressed. The tendency is to move down the ladder, as it were, mission to power, power to structure, structure to resources instead of up the ladder. In Terry's theoretical framework, mission defines the distribution of power, which in turn yields the structure of the organization, and ultimately determines the allocation of resources.

Taking this concept further, there are three areas where mission integration can be demonstrated:

- human resources practices from selection to rewards;
- strategic planning centered on mission fulfillment and synthesizing other analyses;
- organizational integrity and compliance emanating from the mission.

Periodic Mission Assessment and Development Processes serve as opportunities for reviewing and testing this integration as well as for organizational renewal and rededication to the mission.

MISSION AND HUMAN RESOURCES

It should be clear from the preceeding discussion that mission cannot be a mere slogan or motto nicely framed in elevators and the cafeteria or printed on the backs of employee pay checks or badges. It must permeate the organization and all facets of its life and be witnessed by every employee, staff member, faculty, and trustee. Further, all individuals associated with the organization must be able to identify with it. Each must find some alignment or attunement with his or her personal value system for there to be a fit. Clearly then, how well mission is integrated into the human resource function of the organization is an essential factor in successful mission integration.

One of the first steps in integrating mission and human resources is to review all position descriptions for appropriate and measurable mission behaviors and outcomes. Then hiring flows from this description to help assure a fit. When hiring begins with providing prospective candidates with position descriptions that incorporate measurable mission fulfillment expectations appropriate to the role, interviewing and screening for "fit" as well as professional competence, there is mutual understanding of performance expectations.

Employee orientation, rather than being a one-time event, becomes an on-going incorporation into the organization, its history, culture, and mission and values.[4] Further, when these expectations are examined during annual performance reviews, there is continuing reinforcement of the individual's contribution to the mission. Clearly, linking performance expectations, for fulfillment of the mission as well as other organizational measures, with the needed leadership competencies is essential to the task of describing the position in terms of outcome measures. The effort also goes a long way towards describing the desired mission-grounded organizational culture which is a critical component in the assessment of the "fit" of a candidate.

Additionally, when hiring the administrative or executive officer involves board members, as it generally does, orientation of the search committee to mission-based criteria and sensitive screening and interviewing techniques is essential. Board members, coming as many of them do from for-profit and entrepreneurial businesses, may need reassurance in their understanding of the importance of selecting persons capable of personally identifying with the mission and of meeting the expectations of mission fulfillment.

Colleges and universities have more recently engaged in vigorous discussion of mission-based hiring practices. The obvious benefit is that faculty and administrative recruitment efforts would then be able to identify individuals with both professional competence and cultural fit. On many campuses this has been successfully implemented; on others, this has not been the case. In some instances, this initiative has been passionately debated, with questions arising around affirmative action, diversity and ecumenism, academic excellence and academic freedom; the academy's need to sharpen critical thinking and analysis skills, potential conflict with promotion and tenure policies; invasion of privacy. None of these are insurmountable, as several colleges have demonstrated by successfully implementing such policies. Ingredients contributing to successful implementation are the formulation of the questions to be used in the screening and the process of involving faculty in understanding the rationale and in shaping the actual implementation. Rev. James Heft, SM, provost at Dayton University, has done considerable work in this area and describes successful practices in *Current Issues in Catholic Higher Education.*[6]

Organizations which have in a disciplined and focused way performed the task of linking mission and hiring practices and detailing the cultural characteristics, have found them to be extremely rewarding exercises. Not unlike mission assessment processes, the actual implementation of such a practice carries with it benefits to organizational renewal and indirectly to mission education. The process invites individuals to engage in dialogue around what mission integration really is, to envision it concretely, and to articulate it in terms that are tangible and observable. The end result is usually a deeper personal understanding of and commitment to the mission.

The cornerstone of an organization faithful to its mission is the individual who personally embodies and thereby exemplifies the mission and values of the organization, its sponsor, and the Church. It is the individual first and foremost who translates the mission and values into everyday behaviors, who articulates the mission with the core processes of the organization, and who interprets the mission in the light of day-to-day operations. Institutions are only as whole, value-driven, and integrated as the individuals who sponsor, govern, and serve in them. The desire to renew and continually to develop the professionals who serve there and to transform the organization in which they work has lead to serious, disciplined, and focused efforts in integrating mission and human resource functions. Second only to this is the work of creating a mission-driven culture to sustain the efforts.

It is critically important that all persons within the organization live the mission and be held equally and mutually accountable for mission fidelity. When deviant behaviors are overlooked or tolerated, cynicism and disillusionment creep into employee attitudes and erode morale. Mission can and should be imbedded in core practices and processes, but it is the people—faculty, administration, staff, employees, physicians, volunteers— who bring the mission to life within the organization.

While the integration of mission with strategic planning, often referred to as a mission discernment process, is a vital component of the imbedding of mission in an organization, the living witness of the planner, the department chair, the administrator, the finance officer animates and inspires the organization on a day-to-day basis and in turn helps to shape the culture.

Illustrated in Figure 7 are examples of how mission components must be integrated with human resource practices. Two additional practices have been created to bolster and bear responsibility for mission: the creation of mission leadership positions within senior management and the establishment of board level mission committees.

MISSION LEADERSHIP ROLE

In the middle of the 1970's as congregational members began to withdraw from institutional service, particularly senior management positions, sponsoring organizations turned their attention to mission, values integrity, and integration through the creation of senior management positions in the healthcare mission, towards which resources were directed. This practice was later adopted in education. Variously referred to as philosophy, ministerial

Figure 7. Illustration of mission integration with human resource practices

Component	Sample Characteristics/Practices
Fidelity	Commitment to nurturing workplace spirituality; regular use of ritual and reflection; commitment to periodic mission assessment (mission standards, assessment and development process); regular use of mission based decision making processes (mission discernment); mission criteria for staff selection and rewards
Excellence	Systematic approach to measuring and monitoring satisfaction; commitment to performance improvement planning; opportunities for in-service and on-going development; demonstrated commitment to sharing and adopting best practices; universal application of performance standards; commitment to keeping abreast of industry trends, developments
Empowerment	Decisions made at the most appropriate levels; senior leadership visible in the organization; respectful listening and dialogue skills; input solicited and respected; opportunities for spiritual development; commitment to continuous learning
Stewardship	Stewardship understood as more than fiscal stewardship; intangible assets (reputation, legacy, history) stewarded; culture reflects commitment to respect for environment; senior leadership set tone for whole organization's role in stewarding resources

effectiveness, mission effectiveness, apostolic effectiveness, the position reponsible for this generally reported to the CEO or administrator. Needless to say, there was some controversy and debate about the imposition of a new position, about how and who made the appointment, and about the relationship between this position and other roles that related to mission and values. On some fronts there was also a challenge to the very creation and necessity of the role.

There are strong and valid arguments in favor of a senior officer or executive charged with mission responsibilities in religiously sponsored organizations. On the other hand, the counter argument is that everyone needs to be involved in and responsible for mission fulfillment and awareness; ergo, there is no need for a new management role for mission. There is no argument with the statement that mission is everyone's responsibility—so too is financial performance, medical outcomes, and academic excellence. No organization would be without an academic dean or financial officer—regardless of how responsible everyone else in the organization is about financial performance and academic excellence. Should mission receive less attention?

When mission roles were first introduced into religiously sponsored organizations, they were largely filled by members of the sponsoring congregation and most often were second, and sometimes, third careers. Their introduction was not without controversy as noted above, however, and a myriad of questions arose. Could they speak for the congregation? Were they "the sponsor *in situ*"? What qualifications should they possess? Could they come from outside the sponsoring congregation? Could they be lay persons?

Over the three decades since the inception of this role, those questions were largely resolved. They could not speak for the congregation unless specifically directed to do so. They definitely were not the sponsor *in situ*. Their qualifications were gradually identified and classified as the role became more professionally-oriented. Lay persons and religious, possessing the necessary competencies and skills, could fill the roles. In fact, requisite competence and not membership in the congregation should be criteria for appointing mission leadership.

Eventually, the role became more and more defined and several graduate programs were developed to prepare professionals for mission leadership around the country. These were primarily for healthcare ministry although the programs were broadly based and application could be made to other ministries as well. Lay persons began to see this as a valid "career" option and embraced it as a way of serving in a ministry of the Church.

Initially, in the healthcare setting, the mission role threatened both pastoral services (chaplaincy) and human resources. Chaplaincy had long striven for professional recognition, acceptance, and incorporation into the mainstream, particularly in healthcare. They became valued members of the case management team, the ethics committees, and expanded their services to include not only patients/residents and their families but the caregivers as well. Their long sought status seemed to be eclipsed by the creation of senior management positions in mission. In some cases, there was even dispute about where chaplaincy would report—to the mission executive or to patient services. Some chaplains sought professional preparation to change careers and enter the professional role of mission leader. A different circumstance exists in education where human resource departments oversee different activities of the organization and may assist in personal and professional development. In academia this potential for turfism is not so strongly experienced.

In the healthcare setting, human resource staff, emerging as they were from being categorized as personnel, also seemed at times to resent the mission role and its higher ranking in to administrative hierarchy. And when mission began to identify its duties as ministry leadership development, turfism surfaced in some areas. Where the mission role flourished, it was integrally linked into key human resource functions. Mission needed to inform and not be limited to performance management responsibilities such as selection, orientation, development, and evaluation, but also downsizing, lay-offs, and labor relations matters. Hand-in-hand mission and human resources make the difference in shaping and nurturing the culture and climate of the organization.

MISSION COMMITTEES

To further concretize mission integration efforts in governance and to identify a locus for accountability, mission committees of the boards were created. Here, as in other cases cited above, there were questions of its necessity, membership, and objectives. Necessity was raised on the

argument that everyone in every role is concerned about and responsible for mission—why create another body?

Early on the objectives of the committee were not always clearly focused. Should it focus on compliance with "Catholic directives" such as *Ex Corde Ecclesiae* or the *Ethical and Religious Directives*? Should it review campus ministry, chaplaincy, charity care, service learning, and community service (the traditional foci of mission)? Or should it expand its focus and look at hiring policies and practices, mission assessment processes, and other core practices?

A third issue, membership, revolved around the extent to which the sponsoring congregation should be involved. Should they be the majority? Must they come from the campus? From congregational leadership? If the committee were to be populated with a majority of congregational members, did it not defeat the purpose of sharing responsibility for mission fulfillment?

These questions and concerns were helpful in sharpening the focus and objectives in calling for the establishment of such groups. Each organization resolved the matters in ways appropriate to its unique situation, largely reflecting where it was on the continuum of sponsorship evolution or adaptation. Some organizations, after an initial experience with a separate mission committee, disbanded the committee and required the other committees to demonstrate mission integration into its policies and practices, with periodic assessment. In any case, the establishment of mission committees or the integration of mission into the work of all committees did a great service to mission education and awareness.

Mission and Culture

The role of mission and culture, long taken for granted, has recently been more significantly explored. Mission is the source and shaper of organizational culture. It articulates the values and norms by which operations, management, decision-making take place. No one addresses this relationship better than Edgar Schein in most of his writings and studies. There is an unambiguous link between an organization's mission and the espoused culture. When the lived culture departs from the espoused culture, the dysfunction and incongruity are obvious.

In his most recent work, *Primal Leadership*, Daniel Goleman comments on the lack of success of leadership development efforts across the board. Essentially, Goleman concludes that failure in this arena is based on a failure to understand, respect, and reform the culture. "Development alone will not succeed," he contends. Another prominent writer on culture and organizations, James Collins, contends that "a company should not change its core values in response to market changes; rather it should change markets, if necessary, to remain true to its core values."

Creation of a new mission-based culture must be rooted in praxis, theological reflection and action, and conditioned on accountability and community. Without any of the components—theological reflection, accountability, and community—the endeavor, however well-meaning, lacks the internal quality to sustain itself over the long haul. The observable actions and decisions of the organization are the public face of its mission and meaning.

Recalling Terry's framework—mission, power, structure, and resources—one is reminded of the potential power of the mission to align the organization and to be the driver of organizational architecture. When this centrality of mission is realized, the entire culture of the organization—its symbols, language, rituals, practices—reflect or embody the mission.

MISSION DISCERNMENT: MISSION AND STRATEGIC PLANNING

The link between organizational strategic planning and mission can be somewhat challenging to demonstrate, and much less to sell to planners. One often finds that well intentioned planners will lead off a strategic planning efforts with a thoughtful reflection on the mission, only to lay it aside in order to get on with the business of planning. Or, failing to launch planning activities with a look at the mission, there is a tendency to give it a retrospective glance and an "Oh, by the way, how does this relate to the mission?" query. While these two approaches may serve to remind those engaged in the process of the primacy of the mission, they fail to embed mission reflection within the process. The latter is a far more challenging approach.

Trained professionals, planners look to financial pro formas, strategic or market rationale, returns on investment, assets, or equity—and rightly so. Academic planning looks at potential student markets; market competition; accreditation requirements; student-faculty ratios, to name but a few of the normal questions raised in a planning process. Healthcare planners would raise questions of clinical requirements, equipment and capital needs.

When human resource professionals are brought into the planning process, there will also be an analysis of the "people requirements." These range from recruitment and retention of qualified staff and faculty; retraining or upgrading and credentialing staff. Attorneys are expected to bring legal analyses to the table: anti-trust, fraud and abuse, barriers to entry. Often the resultant business plan is a compilation or amalgam of plans. The value a mission-based planning approach can contribute to the process is synthesizing these divergent analyses, and offering a process through which competing interests and goals may be reconciled.

The holism of mission can be the unifying and clarifying lens. It has the power to synthesize all feasibility and analytic studies into a cohesive base for decision-making. ,

Figure 8. USES OF MISSION IN RELATIONSHIP TO PLANNING		
WHEN USED	**HOW USED**	**INTEGRATED USE**
Pre-planning	Opening reflection, inspiration, and set aside	Framework of mission reflection imbedded in process
End stage	Litmus test when plan is complete	Source of post implementation evaluation, based on questions formulated in pre-planning stage

However well meaning, using it as an inspirational piece at the inception of a planning process to set a tone or as a reminder of the organization's fundamental purpose only serves to segregate and fragment mission from the "vital input" into strategic planning and direction setting. Mission must ultimately be at the root of business objectives because it should describe the business purposes and goals and thereby inform and shape business planning and decision-making. The mission **is** the business of the entity.

An example that lays out the usual business objectives side by side with the mission motivation will make these points more clear. Figure 9 focuses on five customary components of a business analysis, with samples of business outcomes or objectives, and in the third column, the mission driver. While the outcomes may be identical, the motivation and the incentive to achieve the outcome is derived from and supports the mission.

The example is only meant to be illustrative of the interrelatedness of traditional business planning tools and mission. The illustration continues to use the example from Holy Cross and similarities with other organizational mission drivers should be self-evident. The core of all organizational mission statements is the Gospel, translated into practical realities of the individual context of the organization.

As examples of mission-based planning, consider the case of the 75 -bed rural, acute care facility challenged by its system / corporate management to significantly improve performance or face sale or closure. The mission of the organization was to bring the healing love of God to all peoples, regardless of creed, race, age, financial resources.

When the board met, under the mandate of the system office to rewrite its strategic plan, the process originally planned included a prayerful reading of the mission followed by traditional discussion of how to increase patient base and payer mix.

It was readily apparent that this method, used repeatedly in the past, would not yield any significantly different results nor guarantee any greater success. Challenged to use the mission statement as a source of "out of the box" thinking as well as inspiration, the board identified several innovative ways to re-imagine and re-create the organization. Mission became not the introduction to the planning process but the source of the new plan itself. As a result of refocusing the planning process, the board was able to consider such innovations as becoming a primary care facility with greater integration with a tertiary facility located elsewhere in the state; becoming a long-term care center; becoming a one-day hospital for minor treatment modalities. All the alternatives are faithful to the mission to bring God's healing love to those being served. The mission-driven process freed the board to see new ways of being true to its founding purpose and still meet community needs, and its system expectations.

From education comes a sterling example when the Jesuit community in Chicago discerned the need to create a secondary school in the Pilsen/Little Village area, a Latino community on the south side of Chicago. The mission statement for the school was to provide Jesuit-Catholic secondary education for the children of first generation Mexican Americans. Three educational planning chal-

Figure 9. Examples of Traditional Business Planning Infused with Mission: The Mission Reflection Process

Area of concern	Objectives	Mission Dimension
Financial requirements and performance	Adequate returns	Stewardship of financial resources
Market growth	Increased market share	Organizational viability
Performance outcomes	Growth, net profits, customer satisfaction, test scores, medical outcomes	Excellence as the hallmark of product and service delivery
Competitive advantage	Market differentiation	Mission-based culture and climate
Human resource requirements	Employee retention; employee satisfaction	Empowerment and stewardship of human resources

lenges immediately emerged from the mission: language (English, Spanish, or both?); tuition and financial support (economically distressed area); and academic skills development (few role models in family or community). Using its mission as the foundation of its planning, Cristo Rey Jesuit High School created a unique and innovative secondary school. Cristo Rey is a dual language school whose curriculum includes actual student employment in entry-level positions in Chicago area businesses to help defray the cost of tuition, and individualized attention to preparing the students for academic success. Ultimately, the school is a phenomenal success and truly faithful to its founding mission.

These examples could be multiplied many times over to illustrate the power of the mission to not only inspire but to infuse the planning process. If one sees every dimension of the organization as an expression of its mission, direction-setting and decision-making can be creatively and faithfully discharged. Lastly, mission criteria, identified in the planning process, can and should become the criteria on which implementation evaluation is based. Therefore, as an integral part of the mission-based planning process, evaluative criteria need to be identified for later use. In this manner, the whole process from inception to assessment is grounded in the mission.

This use of mission as a central driver of the planning process is variously referred to as Mission Discernment, Ethical Reflection, Mission-based Decision-making. It is a rigorous, disciplined process engaged in over a period of time with diverse constituencies participating. Through the process, the social responsibility of the organization as expressed in its mission is assessed in relation to other factors or potential drivers, most notably, who is impacted (positively and negatively) by the potential decision and what self-interests are advanced. Through this rigor, fidelity to mission can be assured.

Again using the example of the four-fold elements—fidelity, excellence, empowerment, and stewardship—some of the discernment questions are illustrated in Figure 10.

By systematically addressing these and similar questions emanating from the mission statement, the potential planning effort intentionally grounds the potential strategy in the mission and values of the organization. Issues that would have a negative impact can be identified before hand and strategies set in place to mitigate any negative results. Additionally, as mentioned earlier, in the assessment process, criteria for post-implementation evaluation should be identified. While the law of unintended consequences can never be fully avoided, such a discernment process sets the bar for performance achievement and seeks to avert negative fallout. No plan is without risk but no plan should put the mission at risk.

MISSION ASSESSMENT AND DEVELOPMENT

One of the richest and most rewarding practices in institutional ministries is that of a periodic mission assessment and development process. Few activities of the organization are as all encompassing, renewing, and energizing as this process. While the results of the assessment lead to a development plan aimed at deepening and enhancing

Figure 10. SAMPLE MISSION DISCERNMENT PROCESS QUESTIONS

Fidelity

What is the impact of this potential initiative on the community being served? How does it affect the poor? Those needing/using the services already?

What are the implications for the Catholic identity of the organization? What are the implications for the sponsors? For the diocese?

Excellence

Can this initiative insure excellence in the product (clinical outcomes, student learning, faculty development)?

Can this initiative insure excellence in the delivery (respect for the dignity or persons, patient, student, customer satisfaction)?

How will the board be assured of ultimate quality/excellence?

Quality measures?

What are any legal issues raised by pursuing this?

Empowerment

What are the credentialing, training, or experience/educational requirements? How would this impact current faculty? Staff? Employees? Physicians?

How does this impact future recruitment and retention?

Stewardship

What economic resources are required?

Does this represent good use/stewardship of financial resources?

Deploying capital or financial resources in this project impacts what other initiatives negatively? What would have to be delayed? Eliminated?

mission fulfillment, it is the process itself that is important. The manner is which such a process is rolled out, the culture and resources of the organization dictate the frequency of its occurrence, and the degree of participation. However, the more individuals who participate, particularly through interdisciplinary teams, the richer the experience. When surgeons sit down with nursing staff, dietary personnel, and security and all share their experiences and expectations of mission fulfillment, what could be a more en-livening and engaging exercise in organizational renewal.

The process of Mission Assessment and Development begins with the articulation of standards or visible, measurable examples of mission fulfillment generally created by teams most directly connected with the area under discussion. For example, creative charity care measures can be identified by the finance office, collections department, social work, emergency departments; one would be surprised what creative approaches can be identified and later celebrated.

Additionally, the mission role gradually expanded to include participation in strategic planning and decision-making. Here, too, the challenge lay in negotiating roles. Many strategic planners had come from for-profit business and industry and the principles guiding decision-making in the not-for-profit, religiously-sponsored world were often foreign to the thinking of such executives. At the same time, mission leaders needed to be at the table in a multi-disciplinary mode—not just of decision-making but also of mission discernment and integration into the process. New tools had to be developed for the process and new skills learned by each party.

Examples of standards or criteria using fidelity, excellence, empowerment, and stewardship are shown in Figure 11.

Mission leadership roles are a recent development in higher education and much can be learned from the experiences of healthcare. As congregational membership and active participation in institutional ministries diminishes, the mission role both in education and in healthcare, is viewed as a critical measure to help insure the continuity of the vision and values of the sponsors. Learnings can be shared across the ministries to enrich the mission development agenda.

Making the Best Use of the Mission Statement

Creating or renewing the mission statement is best done within a theological reflection process. Traditionally, this process has four components: scripture, tradition, experience, and immediate context. Theological reflection is the work of the community involved in the ministry; it is a corporate responsibility and must be a core competence of the organization. In describing contemporary theological reflection, James and Evelyn Whitehead, in their seminal study of theological reflection, ascribe three characteristics to it: portable, performable, and communal.

Theological reflection on mission satisfies all three requirements. Using the example of the four elements from the Holy Cross Mission Statement—fidelity, excellence, empowerment, and stewardship—one can easily see its portability, performability, and applicability to almost any decision-making task. How is this [project, plan, proposal]

Figure 11. MISSION ASSESSMENT AND DEVELOPMENT SAMPLE ITEMS

Fidelity   Employees, faculty, staff know the story of the founding sponsors; Catholic teachings are known and respected; Diocesan relationships are nurtured; Religious beliefs of all are respected; Mission Discernment is evident in all major planning processes and decision-making

Excellence   Periodic review of quality measures includes all involved; Systematic quality improvement projects are implemented as needed; All employees, faculty and staff are annually evaluated on established quality criteria; Service delivery receives equal attention with outcome measures; Satisfaction surveys are reviewed and interventions applied as needed

Empowerment   Turnover rates are reviewed; Diversity initiatives demonstrate respect for other cultures and groups; Development plans with needed resources are available to all; Respect for the dignity of all persons is part of annual review

Stewardship   Periodic reminders and examples of environmental stewardship are evident; Fiscal stewardship is defined as everyone's responsibility; All assume stewardship of intangible assets: history, reputation, legacy of the organization

consistent with the organization's founding vision and values? To what degree can excellence in service and outcomes be attained? Who is impacted positively?—Negatively? And what resources will be required and where do they come from?

Depending on the circumstances, the reflection can be individual or communal. All major decision-making processes require the input of multiple disciplines and they are usually iterative—building on prior, intermediate reflective processes. Today's environment is so complex and challenging that multiple perspectives are essential to good decision-making and no less so for theological reflection. When the chief financial officer voices the question, "Does this really fit our mission?" one can be assured mission is permeating the ranks of the leadership.

MISSION AND THE CREATION OF A COMMUNITY OF COMMITTED PERSONS

One of the more critical needs in institutional ministries today is the need for community within the workplace and a deeper understanding of a theology of the common good.

Businesses and industries promote communities of practice, learning communities, places where individuals can come together to share best practices, learnings, explore new ways of thinking and serving. These communities are intentional in that they are created with specific interests or objectives in mind. They are often stronger and more lasting than work teams which tend to be focused on a single objective or task and disband when the particular goal was reached. The communities envisioned here are multi-disciplinary, like the mission assessment teams, with a commitment to each other and the end, in this case, mission fidelity. They also hold one another accountable.

Only through the creation of communities of persons—persons serving in sponsorship roles, persons leading and governing the institutions, and persons serving in any capacity in the organization—will the full realization of mission integration be possible. Anything less betrays the vision of the founding sponsors and denies those involved with the opportunity of advancing the reign of God. In responding to the call to serve the organization's mission individuals touch into their deepest selves and truly become "partners in this between time."

Questions for Reflection

- To what extent does mission not only influence but infuses our decision-making processes?

- To what extent foes the annual budget and calendar reflect our organizational mission?

- Can every security guard and surgeon, every professor and print shop worker quote our mission and values? If not, where would they find it?

- To borrow an image from Thomas Berry, is our mission the prism through which our works shine? or is it the other way around, are our works the prism through which the mission is refracted?

PART III

REFLECTIONS ON MISSION AND ORGANIZATIONAL INTEGRITY

BY JOHN A. GALLAGHER, PhD

"At the still point of the turning world. Neither flesh nor fleshless;
Neither from nor towards; at the still point, there the dance is,
But neither arrest nor movement. And do not call it fixity,
Where past and future are gathered. Neither movement from nor towards
Neither ascent nor decline. Except for the point, the still point,
There would be no dance, and there is only the dance.
I can only say there we have been: but I cannot say where.
And I can not say how long, for that is to place it in time."[12]

—T.S. Eliot, " The Four Quartets"

T. S. Eliot's lyrical expression captures the spirit of the themes discussed in previous parts of this work. The premise of each part has been that for religious, laity, and bishops alike, contemporary discussions and conceptions of sponsorship occur in the between time, a period ambiguously located between a well-known and well-traveled past and a future whose social structures and theological convictions remain in part unknown. In Eliot's image the notion of sponsorship is at the still point of the dance, the crescendo of the music from which dénouement and resolution will flow. Theological reflection in the between time must discern what is coming forward from the history of sponsored ministries and then the manner in which the acquired wisdom of our ecclessial history can form fitting adaptations to the religious, economic, social, and cultural particularities in which sponsored ministries can fully mediate their mission. This reflection will outline three components of an evolving notion of sponsorship: institutions, mission, and the moral agency of institutions.

INSTITUTIONS

Throughout its history the Church has developed a variety of sponsored ministries each of which is an expression of the healing ministry of Jesus. In the contemporary American Church, these ministries are collectively referred to as Catholic social services, Catholic education and Catholic healthcare. One of the principal abiding characteristics of these ministries is that they have been conducted in institutional settings. Such sponsored ministries were not principally the work of individuals who provided good works on behalf of the poor, the disenfranchised, the uneducated or the sick. Rather they were the work of women or men bound together in a way of life and dedicated to the creation and maintenance of social structures to meet the social, educational and health needs of members of the communities they served.

In his *Models of the Church*, Avery Dulles identified the Church as institution as one of its basic images, a representation that constitutes an understanding of one of the Church's basic characteristics.[13] The Church is not just a collection of individuals who have received the Gospel's call to repentance and the disemination of the Good News, but rather a society organized and structured to mediate the Word of God to each successive generation. Thus it is consistent with this fundamental characteristic of the Church that it would organize its ministries in an institutional social structure. As Brian Hehir has commented, "The Church is institutional by instinct and by nature."[14]

That the contemporary ministries of the Church are expressed in the institutional structures of schools, welfare organizations, and hospitals is hardly surprising. These institutional ministries are our inheritance from earlier generations that created them and nurtured them into the present. Yet from where we stand today, in the Between Time, institutions can seem alienating. Do schools educate? Do hospitals care? Are welfare institutions responsive to human need or simply another bureaucracy? Secular institutions such as Enron and Arthur Andersen are alleged to have deceived employees, stockholders and others who relied upon them as truth tellers. The between time needs to be characterized, at least in part, as a time in which all persons in society depend upon institutions for their welfare and security and yet there is increasing skepticism whether contemporary institutions mediate the social goods they were created to provide. Indeed one of the major challenges for the Church's sponsored ministries is to overcome such skepticism regarding its own institutions.

From a sociological perspective, institutions are mediating organizations that exist in the gap between macro-organizations such as governments and micro-entities such as the family and individuals. These mediating institutions supply the goods and services essential to human flourishing. They provide food and transportation, education, and health services. Some institutions within American capitalism establish systems for banking, investment, and manufacturing. Most institutions within American society are secular and for profit, they constitute what we refer to colloquially as "corporate America." Collectively, the institutions of American society constitute the system through which families and individuals have access to the goods and services essential to human well-being. Given their significance for the common good of any society, the risk that the skepticism mentioned above poses to any community should be readily apparent. Every society depends upon institutions for its vital, social, and cultural needs.

Institutions and corporations have complex purposes or objectives that they seek attain, goals frequently expressed in mission statements. On one level, their goals are the foods or soaps, cars or wash machines they offer for sale. On another level, they seek profits for investors. On yet another level they seek to secure job security for their staff and employees. In addition, most corporations intend

Partners in the Between Time

to be good citizens, to abide by the law, and to make contributions to beneficent organizations in the community. The key point, however, is that in striving to pursue these objectives, corporations embody values. Their goods and services are safe or lacking in some way. Advertising is a fair representation of the product offered for sale or it is not. Companies take due precautions to protect the job security of employees or they are callous in the manner they deal with employees. Inherent in the life of American institutions is that they mediate values or disvalues. These values or disvalues, more over, are concrete, they are present in the day to day activities of these organizations.

The sociologist Philip Selznick has commented that "Institutions embody value, but they do so as operative systems or going concerns. The trouble is that what is good for the operative system does not necessarily serve the standard or ideals the institution is supposed to uphold. Therefore institutional values are always at risk."[15] As complex entities, organizations can focus on one goal, profit, and lose their focus on competing goals of quality or service. Their attention can become exclusively devoted to one aspect of their operation while other systems begin to malfunction and thus to mediate disvalues. A primary responsibility of corporate boards is to ensure that management is exercising appropriate attention to each aspect of a corporation's operations. The disvalues stemming from institutions are not necessarily the result of the pernicious intentions of managers, but they are more frequently the result of the fact that some aspect of a complex organization has begun to perform poorly.

Catholic theology has consistently stressed the importance of mediating institutions. Indeed, within the tradition the word "institution" has always had the connotation suggested above. Institutions were deemed to be social organizations that produced goods and services essential for human well-being; they, rather than the labor or individuals, were deemed to be the primary source of the common good. But the Latin word "institutio" also had a variety of related connotations. The *Institutiones theologiae moralis* were the books used to educate generations of seminarians in Catholic moral theology. In this context, "institution" pertains to a body of teaching, a body of ethical knowledge. But *institutiones* also suggest a set of norms by which people should live as well as the religious, social, and cultural norms of a society. Thus the social institutions of a society—its schools, corporations, and hospitals—were construed as mediating the norms by which people should live, the religious, social, and cultural norms of society. The contributions of institutions to society, according to this view, are not just limited to the production of goods or services, are not just focused on their constitutive role in the maintenance of the common good of a society, but also extends to their role in maintaining the moral order. As bearers of the religious, social, and cultural values of society, institutions ought to provide the context and support for the moral behavior of individuals within society. It would be naïve to suggest that contemporary American society would, or should, ever regain the ethical homogeneity that this notion of "institutions" suggests. But it would be equally naïve to deny the risk posed to our way of life if we fail to attend to the importance of institutions as mediating values as well as goods and services into our communities.

If the sponsored ministries of the Church are to retain their integrity they must address their role not only in terms of providing quality social services, education, and healthcare, they must equally attend to their roles as mediators of values and disvalues into the communities they serve. It was precisely their role as mediators of values to the community that constituted the distinctive characteristic of these ministries. Whether one refers to it as "Catholic identity," "mission" or the charism of a foundress, within these related notions the distinctive character of the institutional ministries of the Church was birthed. The challenge to contemporary institutional ministries is to retrieve this distinctive character from within our past and to reframe and rethink them for a world which is more secular and pluralistic.

MISSION

The mission of a sponsored ministry is the source of its vitality and purpose. In its written form, a mission statement may emphasize a link to the religious congregation that founded and governed the institutions from its inception to the present. Other mission statements may draw on their linkage to the institutional Church and stress the Catholic identity of the organization. Still other mission statements may draw upon the charism of the foundress of a religious institute or the inspiration of a major administrator within its history. Although the verbal expression of a mission statement is important, what is critical is the manner in which it directs and influences the complex activities of the institution. The mission of the institution is not what is printed on wall hangings and reproduced on laminated cards. The mission of a sponsored ministry is its ensoulment, its animation, its vitality.

The first function of an institution's mission is to define its basic purpose, what it is committed to achieve. Like the missions of its secular counter-parts, the mission of a sponsored ministry defines its core business. The mission of a Catholic hospital distinguishes it from the mission of a social service organization or an educational institution. Mission statements in Catholic healthcare generally allude to the healing ministry of Jesus or the healing ministry of the Church. These basic statements of the fundamental purposes of the institution are then frequently adumbrated with terms such as "excellence," "fidelity," "stewardship," "compassion," and "clinical excellence." Such modifiers of the core business express the manner in which the institution is committed to conducting its core activity. Such qualifying characteristics of the ministry suggest the values it intends to mediate to the community, the meanings of trust, care, and responsibility it strives to engender in the community. The task for sponsors and mission executives is to ensure that such statements in fact animate and reflect the day to day activities of the sponsored institution.

Second, when mission is ensouled in a sponsored ministry it provides the organization with its self-identity. The self-identity of an institution is the product of its core purpose, its history of service in a community, and the oral traditions of the organization. The self-identity of an institution is more than its purpose. The history of an organization, its successes, struggles, and even failures are defining elements in what it is. The history of a sponsored ministry is frequently transmitted through oral traditions, stories in which organizational accomplishments and the deeds of courageous leaders are recalled to sustain the current self-identity of the organization. Such a history provides the organization with its public reputation, how the organization is perceived by the community, patients, and competitors. Authentic self-identity is not proclaimed by its owner but rather conferred by a community.

But is it really logically correct to attribute terms such as "self-identity" and "ensoulment" to organizations? When organizations are discussed as persons, it is only in a metaphorical sense, and it usually remains unclear in what precise sense an organization is like a person. Certainly they do not have intellectual or volitional capacities as constitutive elements of their definition. In fact institutions are really not very much like persons at all. Probably the only reason we think of organizations as persons is because the law creates the legal fiction of the corporation as a person before the law.

There are, however, two reasons that make it possible to attribute self identity and ensoulment to sponsored institutional ministries. First, organizations and institutions have cultures. The culture of an organization is a historically transmitted pattern of meanings that sustain institutional self-identity and purpose. Organizational culture forges the multitude of persons and the vast variety of tasks that need to be accomplished into a relatively effective whole. Culture is not abstract, rather it is the concrete, explicit set of assumptions, presuppositions, expectations, and anxieties that govern strategic and operational decisions within an organization. The professionalism of the medical staff, nurses, and management are also constituent components of the culture of a healthcare organization, just as the administration, faculty, and staff of an educational institution is.

The written mission statement is a verbal expression of an element of the culture. So also the policies and procedures are written expressions of operational dimensions of the culture. Organizational culture changes as better ways of doing things are learned and because legal, social, and economic developments require change. Although culture is as concrete as the day-to-day operations and decisions on a sponsored ministry, it is at the same time extremely difficult to capture the whole of a culture in words.

The second reason that sponsored ministries can be described as ensouled, as having purpose and self-identity is that they are nothing more than human creations sustained by on-going human activities. Remove the people from an institution and what remains is an empty building, perhaps of some historical or anthropological interest. Founders and early participants in a sponsored ministry established over time an institutional culture; their successors maintain and recast the culture through the decisions they make or avoiding making. Institutions are not natural products, there is no absolute necessity about them, they are neither inherently good nor inherently evil. Institutions are effective or ineffective, capable of sustaining the common good or become threats to the common good only because of the decisions made by persons inside them or because of the demands or expectations of the society in which they exist. Although frequently large and complex there is no inevitability to their success or failure.

MORAL AGENCY

In *Models of the Church*, Dulles characterizes the Church not only as institution, but also as servant and herald.[16] As servant, the Church is in ministry to the world, a ministry of *deaconia*. Through its service to the world, the Church is in service to spiritual and other human needs. In this dimension of its ministry the Church meets the world were it is with its social and economic systems that sustain or cripple the common good. Here the Church engages the world's morality and immorality, its surfeit of goods and its devastating poverty. At the same time that the Church is servant to the world, it is also herald. As herald the Church bears witness to Gospel values and to the moral principles enunciated in the tradition. Through its institutional sponsored ministry the Church encounters the world as both servant and herald. Thus the sponsored ministries of the Church not only bear the model of the Church as institution, but also as servant and herald. From an ecclesiological perspective sponsored ministries bear the constitutive marks of institution, servant, and herald.

There is an inherently creative tension that sponsored ministries experience in their roles as servant and as herald. As servant, healthcare, education, and social service ministries encounter not the world, but a community with its needs and desires, its culture, its economic, social, and legal systems. The ministry engages these systems by treating patients, teaching students, servicing clients, seeking accreditation, ensuring that best practices are studied and followed. In the very same encounters in which the ministry strives to be a servant, it also must be a herald, its must strive to maintain its fidelity to the values of the Gospel. Therein lies the fundamental tension inherent in healthcare as a sponsored ministry of the Church. This tension is irreducible, it cannot be eliminated or resolved. In a discussion of this tension, Dulles has suggested that the Church should "enter into critical dialogue with contemporary cultures, accepting what is sound, opposing what is faulty, and attempting to supply what is lacking."[17] The task of negotiating this tension is the most fundamental mission responsibility of a Catholic organization and thus is a fundamental responsibility of sponsors and mission executives.

The management of this tension reveals the moral agency of a sponsored ministry. The moral agency of sponsored ministries is responsive. Institutions rarely create initiatives *de novo*, rather they respond to changes in their enviornment. Changes in the market, developments in medical science and technology, new expectations of payors as well as evolving community expectations are examples of events that evoke the moral agency of institutions.

The responses of a sponsored ministry are the result of processes. Organizations analyze data, they review the same data from different perspectives. Financial and legal implications need to be assessed, as do the operational and human resource dimensions of an impending decision. Strategic decisions may evaluate possible impact on the community and potential reactions from competitors. Such work employs the skills and expertise of management. The various analyses are developed in the functional divisions of the organization and then brought together in a unified manner for presentation to senior management, the board, and sponsors. The response-making capacity of an organization entails multiple coordinated processes.

What can be overlooked in these multiple analyses is the ethical dimension of an impending response. Attached to each phase and level of analysis there needs to be a discernment process that will bring into consideration the ethical dimension latent in many institutional decisions. This is a skill that the professional preparation of many healthcare managers does not provide them. The issue is not the personal moral sensitivities of managers, nor that if an ethical issue were brought to their attention they would fail to address it. Rather the issue is that they are not trained to identify them. Ethical issues or arbitrating the tensions in their organization between its role as servant and herald are not issues with which they are comfortable.

There are a variety of ways to introduce discernment into the analytical processes of a sponsored ministry. Processes can be devised that can facilitate the identification of ethical issues. General questions can be formulated which probe for potential ethical problems and that guide managers to where to look and what to look for. A competency can be developed among managerial staff that will enable them to identify ethical issues, encourage them to discuss such issues in committee meetings, and to document them in minutes and reports. However an organization goes about the process of managing the tension between its roles as servant and herald, it must do so in a manner that ensures that its responses serve the mission of the sponsored ministry.

The point of these multiple analytical processes is not just to identify problems, but even more so to initiate the formulation of a fitting response. A response is the result of management's intentional consideration of an issue and the formulation of how the organization will respond. Responses are not ready made, frequently they are not generalizable. Responses are crafted to meet the exigencies of a unique array of circumstances in a particular community and they are crafted in a manner that maintains the tension between an organization's roles as servant and herald. Fitting responses are intended to be congruent with the mission, culture, and self-identity of a sponsored ministry, but also to be congruent to the needs of a variety of stakeholders. Fitting responses are the outcome of the multiple levels and types of analysis organizations employ in the resolution of an issue.

Conclusion

In the between time one should look to retrieve from the past those elements that can contribute to contemporary foundations for the ministry. Clearly the ministry will retain each of its ecclesiological characteristics as institution, servant, and herald. As institutional ministries of the Church, Catholic organizations will continue to be accountable for the goods and services they provide to the common good of a community as well as for their roles as mediators of moral values. They will need to manage their roles of servant and herald in ethical, social, and cultural environments that is heterogeneous and complex. They will need to develop analytical processes that will enable them to discern to accept what is sound, oppose what is faulty, and supply what is lacking.

Partners in the Between Time

PART IV

REFLECTIONS FROM HIGHER EDUCATION

CONTRIBUTED BY SUSAN SANDERS, RSM, PhD AND
KAYE ASHE, OP, PhD

*It is the honor and responsibility of a Catholic university to consecrate
itself without reserve to the cause of truth.*
—Pope John Paul II

THE INCREASING INVOLVEMENT OF THE LAITY

In Catholic higher education, "between time" is marked with many of the changes and developments described earlier in this volume. The trend toward the growing presence and influence of the laity in this sector which began in the 1960s is now a well-established and accepted fact. Virtually every Catholic college or university is governed by a lay Board of Trustees, even while its sponsorship typically resides with the founding religious congregation. Further, its highest administrative posts and the majority of its faculty positions are filled by the laity.

This increase in the influence of the laity has caused concern among the hierarchy. While it is difficult to document, Church authorities seem to suspect that the commitment of lay leaders to their training in Church teaching might not be as strong as that of the men and women religious founders and sponsors whose formal and canonical connection to the hierarchical Church is closer and more direct.

This transfer of responsibility from religious congregations to the laity paralleled that which took place earlier in elementary schools, in other Catholic social service agencies, and in Catholic healthcare. Interestingly, few in the hierarchical Church seemed as worried about the erosion of Catholic identity in these institutional ministries as they are now worried about the Catholic identity of our colleges and universities and our sponsored healthcare institutions. Apparently, there is an assumption that these institutions have a special responsibility to maintain and defend values traditionally held by the Church. The fact that these ministries are also highly visible and command huge commitments of financial resources to maintain, however, cannot be ignored. It will be the task of the contemporary American Church, and to some extent, the sponsoring religious congregations, to resolve whatever tensions remain between a concerned hierarchy and the increasing diversity of the trustees, administration, faculty, and student bodies of Catholic institutions of higher education.

The Integration of Catholic Higher Education into the American Academy

Catholic colleges and universities, like their secular counterparts, bring the best and the brightest to faculties, classrooms, and research labs. Many faculty members hold doctoral degrees from nationally regarded Research I institutions. They come with high expectations in regards to teaching and research. Moreover, they are generally highly enthusiastic and expert in their disciplines and methodologies.

Sometimes, however, doctoral disciplinary training excludes consideration of the contribution of other disciplines, especially those that are non-empirically based. For example, it is not unusual for those in the physical and social sciences to be skeptical about the contribution of the discipline of theology to intellectual discourse. Consequently, the theological, faith, or religious dimensions of questions and the research associated with them, perhaps appreciated as argument, are often ignored, discounted, or even disdained. Even while some scholars value the study of *how* people behave when they profess belief in God, they nevertheless may deem it intellectually irrelevant or unimportant to study the linkage between one's belief and one's behaviors that are based on the belief *that* God exists and is involved in our lives. After all, God's existence cannot be proved using the empirical methods that many academicians typically rely on in their research.

In such cases, one's disciplinary training or methodological bias may actually limit rather than broaden a search for truth because it cannot admit of theological realities. Further, such a bias may also persist to the point where members of the academy refuse to recognize or even tolerate the positions of scholars who would dare to argue the religious dimensions of any question or issue. In this regard, some members of the academy may ironically become impediments to the very broad search for truth based on the melding faith and reason that John Paul II advocates in *Ex Corde Ecclesiae*.

THE EFFECTS OF INCREASING DIVERSITY AND PLURALISM

Catholic colleges and universities have always been graced by the teaching and scholarship of non-Catholic colleagues. The contributions of these colleagues have been especially evident as their presence in Catholic higher education has dramatically increased during the late 20th century. In part, the growing religious pluralism—and even the increasing ethnic and racial diversity—in our faculties derive from the need to teach a less Eurocentric curriculum. Globalization and the fact that Vatican II promoted ecumenism and interfaith dialogue also un-doubtedly drove efforts to recruit a more diverse faculty. To support a broad curriculum that addresses global issues, for example, we need to recruit faculty who under-stand Eastern non-Christian religions.

The presence of such colleagues results in better teaching, better discourse, and better understanding across religions, races, and ethnicities. This is crucial in an age when peace among individuals and groups, not to mention world peace, depends on such understanding. Neverthe-less, some construe such a diversification of faculty and staff as being tantamount to a dilution of our Catholic identity. How can a university's Catholic identity be enhanced, some ask, when there are proportionately fewer Catholics teaching and serving at our universities? Why, some have complained, isn't the chair of a theology or religious studies department a Catholic? Why does a university support the prayer and rituals of those who are non-Catholic—or even non-Christian?

College or university faculties are not the only campus groups to experience a growing pluralism. The racial, ethnic, economic, and religious profiles of our student bodies are also becoming more diverse. For a variety of reasons, including philosophical, pedagogical, and financial pressures, Catholic colleges and universities have reached out to international students and to local students from different religious traditions. These students, as well as those adults returning to college to complete degrees, helped swell enrollments at many Catholic colleges and universities.

Thus, even as the faculties of these institutions began to diversify, so did the racial, religious, cultural, and ethnic compositions of our student bodies. As the proportion of Catholic students decreased relative to the number of other students who profess other or no religious beliefs, the Catholic character appeared, to some, to wane.

Moved by the spirit of ecumenism, and even by the words of *Ex Corde* itself, Catholic colleges and universities now increasingly try to support the religious and spiritual needs of non-Catholic students, as well as the spiritual life of non-Christians. As Catholic campus ministers, for example, respond to the needs of Catholic students for Catholic liturgical, sacramental, worship, and service opportunities, they also offer non-Catholic students the campus space and the university resources to conduct their own religious services on campus.

Adopting such an approach sometimes results in controversy over such issues as whether nondenominational ways of praying—or non-Christian forms of addressing the God—should substitute for uniquely Catholic expressions, signs, and symbols. Should, for example, the invocation at commencement be a generic prayer that acknowledges a non-denominational God? Should the prayer refer to Jesus explicitly, thereby taking on an expressly Christian dimension? Should the ceremony and prayer end with the Sign of the Cross, a uniquely Catholic expression of faith?

Responses that are not uniquely Catholic to an increasingly pluralistic campus community are evident not only in the programs and approaches of campus ministers and student affairs personnel but also in the faculty's questions about what courses should be included in the undergraduate general education program. Should every student be required to take common core *theology* classes, for example, in sacramental, moral, or fundamental theology? Is the move away from theology departments and toward departments of religious studies a good one? Is it possible to maintain one's mission and Catholic identity by allowing students to fulfill theology requirements in a generic way, for example, by taking classes in comparative religions? Or by substituting a philosophy class for a theology or religious studies course? Or by offering opportunities to study non-Christian or non-Western religions without learning anything about Church history and Catholic social teaching? Or should students be required to take any theology or religious studies courses at all?

Questions of Catholic identity and religious pluralism arise in other academic areas as well. Should universities, for example, adopt policies that limit a student's choice of internships or clinical placements because the placement site engages in activities that do not support Catholic teaching?

The presence or absence of uniquely Catholic signs, symbols, and liturgical practices has also sparked conversations. While few faculty would dispute the right of a Catholic university to hold Catholic worship services, some would contend that placing a crucifix or cross in a classroom violates the academic freedom of their classrooms.

Catholic identity issues may become even thornier when inviting speakers to campus, especially when their viewpoints, whether personal or public, do not, in part or in toto, support Catholic doctrine or teaching. The presence of such a speaker—irrespective of the topic he or she is addressing and whether he or she serves in a public or private capacity—some challenge, signal the university's tacit support for positions contrary to the Church? Or, in providing access to and discussion with such a speaker, is the university simply fulfilling what John Paul II describes as its vocation: "to unite existentially by intellectual effort two orders of reality that too frequently tend to be placed in opposition as though they were antithetical: the search for truth, and the certainty of already knowing the fount of truth"?[18]

For those who do not believe that a Catholic university should be involved in the type of dialectical discourse that John Paul II proposes, or who regard Church teaching as static rather than, as most theologians understand it, evolving in response to the times and the experiences of the faithful, then perhaps such speakers should be peremptorily excluded from any campus venue. For those, however, who believe that Catholic colleges and universities are the places where "the Church does its thinking,"[19] or who subscribe to John Paul II's belief that "It is the honor and responsibility of a Catholic university to consecrate itself without reserve to the *cause of truth,*"[20] or who believe that a Catholic university should, "with enthusiasm," be "completely dedicated to the research of all aspects of truth in their essential connection with the supreme Truth, who is God,[21] then such discourse is not only welcomed at Catholic universities but encouraged as a way to fulfill both its vocation and its mission.

Despite the fact that such discourse is intrinsic to the vocation of a Catholic university, engaging in it can nevertheless be costly. These costs may include the withdrawal of financial support for the university, or public protests by angry community members, university constituents, or church-related groups. In their enthusiastic support for a single issue of Church teaching, these protestors seek to limit access to those whose positions differ, even if such positions are not the primary focus of the discussion. Nevertheless, Catholic colleges and universities must engage such positions, informing the debate with faith perspectives, and accurately representing Church teaching where it is relevant. Only through such a dialogical and discursive process can truth be discovered and the meaning of that truth be acted on in a way that promotes knowledge of God and the reign of peace and justice that the Gospels proclaim.

Upholding the value of academic freedom, whether inside or outside the classroom, should not discourage such discussion, but rather, promote it. Both outside and inside the classroom, a Catholic university is in keeping with its educational mission when it protects an intellectual free zone where all perspectives—including secular, religious, and specifically Catholic views—may be freely presented and debated. Catholic colleges and universities that promote a religious ethos or identity through the use of Catholic signs, symbols, and rituals, whether inside the classroom or outside of it, do not impede academic freedom. Rather, they present additional opportunities for study and discussion about the types of faith-based perspectives that can inform intra- and extra-classroom academic discourse.

The infusion of such perspectives, where appropriate, into classroom conversations, does not constrain academic freedom or the search for truth. Nor should it be an attempt, veiled or otherwise, to establish theological litmus tests for the teaching and learning that take place in the Catholic higher education community. Teaching, disciplinary training, and discourse, informed by faith perspectives where appropriate, and set in the context of facilities whose "look" supports awareness of faith perspectives, do not limit academic freedom. Instead, the value of academic freedom is upheld and even strengthened because it challenges those in the academy to be even more expansive in this pursuit of truth.

Educators are always challenged to learn about and to respect traditions and beliefs that differ from our own, even as we sometimes need to insist on positions or take actions that stand in opposition to mainstream thinking, whether inside or outside the campus. This is the struggle of the intellectual life, especially one informed by faith. The benefit of such a struggle, however, has undoubtedly enriched not only understandings of our disciplines but also our understanding of our Catholic identity and our Catholic faith.

The gray areas of the Catholic intellectual life cannot be permanently proscribed, prescribed, or negotiated away, even by policy statements from the hierarchical Church, or university sponsors, trustees, or administrators. Instead, civil, focused, and ongoing discussion around such gray is preferable to the implementation of general norms or policies that try to dictate who will engage in such conversations and under what terms. Such discussion makes a university a university, and makes a Catholic university, as an agent of the Church, a place where "Catholic teaching and discipline are to influence all university activities, while the freedom of conscience of each person is to be fully respected."[22]

Even as sponsors, trustees, administrators, faculty, and staff engage in debate, unfortunately fewer and fewer of our students, including those coming from 12 years of Catholic elementary and secondary schooling, attend religious services or other opportunities for prayer and religious celebration. Increasingly, these come to Catholic higher education as "unchurched," that is, as having no basic understanding of the Catholic Church, its history, its teachings, its practices, or its sacramental life. Our local parishes experience the same phenomenon. College students are conspicuously absent from parish worship services, even when the students live at home. These parishes, however, are not accused of losing their Catholic identity because proportionately fewer college age Catholic students attend worship services. Nor has the Vatican sought to institute general norms to help these parishes recover it. Rome is, apparently, more confident of its ability to command the loyalty of its priests and pastors than it is of controlling belief and practice on Catholic campuses.

EVOLVING NOTIONS OF CATHOLIC IDENTITY

Having evolved toward a broader expression of its mission, but situated in an increasingly secular and religiously pluralistic context, will institutions still be able to maintain their Catholic identity? Although competing notions of Catholic identity have been around since the 1970's, the ground has shifted considerably, as has the discourse about religion, its role in society, and the way it should or should not be expressed in public forums.

To appreciate the distance we have traveled between these shifting, if not competing notions, it is instructive to see how the Reverend Alfred McBride, a Norbertine religious educator, framed the question of Catholic identity in the 1970s. McBride acknowledged the benefits of ecumenism and the fresh air that blew through the Church during the Second Vatican Council. Yet he argued that if the word "Catholic" were to have meaning in terms not only describing a faith tradition, then we must define the limits of ecumenical discussion. Dialogue should consider papal infallibility, the Eucharist, all sacraments, the role of the institutional Church, apostolic succession, miracles, heaven, hell, saints, devils, angels, Sabbath Mass obligation, fasting, abstinence, sexual sins, sins of any kind, and grace. He suggested that questions on these issues, posed with the aim of deciding what distinguishes Catholics from everyone else, should, once and for all, help us define our Catholic identity.

Such an approach may interest few. However, it utterly fails to engage most of us. In fact, we are keenly conscious today that the search for our Catholic identity must not become a labeling device for purposes of easy inclusion and exclusion. Universities, above all, cannot be obsessed with the question of what can or cannot be tolerated as proper positions on the questions outlined above or on other, even more sensitive issues.

The attempt to articulate a set of beliefs and values that are unique to the Catholic community, and thus can serve as a litmus test for Catholicity, would result not in correction of the tendency to drift, but in paralysis. Further, claiming our Catholic identity does not have to do with inward gazing and a possible re-erection of barriers, but with the exercise of spiritual and moral leadership on the questions we face in our age.

John Paul II has called on Catholic educators and institutions to exercise this kind of leadership and to be individual and institutional agents of social justice. Still, the norms he proposes in the second part of *Ex Corde Ecclesiae* seem to suggest that a litmus test is a good way to ensure Catholic identity. We have seen that John Paul II has proposed that, when possible, the president be a Catholic, that Catholics should dominate the membership of boards of trustees (as they already do, in many cases), and that new faculty be Catholic.

If rigorously implemented, such norms and guidelines would function as litmus tests, even if not intended as such. They could, for example, preclude the employment and appointment of nonbelievers—and even other non-Catholic Christians—to our faculties and boards. The norms will not ensure, however, that those who name themselves as baptized Catholics will either believe in or practice the tenets of their faith. On the other hand, the norms may effectively exclude people of other faith traditions who are knowledgeable about and respectful of the Catholic tradition.

Similar concerns arise in regard to the *mandatum* required to teach Catholic studies. Although the faculty member may receive the bishop's approval, having a mandatum will not necessarily ensure that the professor respects, holds, or even faithfully teaches the doctrine or dogma. At best, a *mandatum* makes faithful teaching *possible*. At worst, it may simply discourage good and practicing Catholic scholars from applying for positions in Catholic colleges and universities because they can teach their discipline in secular institutions without being encumbered by the approval processes or potential intellectual limits that a *mandatum* imposes.

The preceding analysis focuses on teachers, administrators, and trustees. What affect might the implementation of these norms have on students, the development of their faith, or the character of their behavior? And how might their behavior reflect a strong Catholic tradition and identity at our institutions of higher education? Will a university's adherence to the general norms effect a dramatic increase in student attendance at Mass? Can we expect that the implementation of the norms will promote both the presence and understanding of Catholic symbols and rituals? Will they guide campus ministers as they try to serve the needs of a student body that is increasingly diverse in its religion? Will they make "unchurched" students more knowledgeable or interested in learning about their faith and the active role that God plays in their lives?

The links are tenuous between the norms that presumably give us our Catholic identity and the desired behavior of the members of our campus communities. Granted, there is some link between what we teach and how we behave, and what students learn from us and from each other. Norms that focus on teacher qualifications and background may have some impact on how students learn, what they value, and how they behave. But even the most sanguine among us knows that a professor is only one influence among many others. Thus, the link between the norms and their desired outcomes is weak at best. Norms will do little to "force" integrity on those professors who are too lazy, too ideological, too angry, or too incompetent to accurately or objectively represent the history and positions of the subjects they teach, even those related to something as fundamental to the university's mission as its faith tradition. Norms that focus on teachers, therefore, may have some impact on how Catholic a university looks and how "Catholic" its students behave. However, they will do little to enhance the ethos of a Catholic university and how it interprets its mission of teaching, research, and service. For this to happen, other strategies are needed.

A Different Perspective on Indicators of Catholic Identity

If the norms John Paul II proposes in *Ex Corde Ecclesiae* are difficult to implement, of dubious efficacy, and possibly an impediment to attracting faithful and strong Catholic presidents, trustees, and faculty members, then what might we do to make a greater impact on the ethos of our institutions? What might we do to make our colleges and universities not only more identifiably Catholic, but also more willing to engage in the pursuit of a vibrant future for the Church?

David J. O'Brien, a Catholic layman and historian at the College of the Holy Cross, argues, "Catholic colleges should continue to seek a renewal of their historic effort to integrate faith and learning, not by reclaiming the institution, but by persuading colleagues and the public that this is a worthwhile thing to do together."[23] Thus, Catholic identity today should not be so much a preoccupation with power and control, as a concern about fidelity to a religious heritage and an educational mission.

Recognizing that, as in all dialectics, we will advance through apparent contradiction to our own completion, we propose three strategies that might help negotiate current tensions about a waning Catholic identity. First, we need to be clear about the knowledge and expectations that our faculty and staff members—especially our new hires—have about the history and purpose of Catholic higher education. Second, we need to critique the content of the curricula, especially the general education curricula, that we offer in view of an incarnational theology that emphasizes that God's love for us has been made incarnate in Jesus whose life challenges us to virtue, to justice, to reconciliation, and to peace. Third, we need to re-think our role as institutional actors within our local communities and in our Church.

CLARIFYING EXPECTATIONS OF FACULTY AND STAFF

Whether or not a faculty or staff member is a believer in a specific religious tradition, the Catholic college or university community must approach each person from a base of trust and the conviction that we are true partners. To establish the principles of partnership, we need to discuss how human and humane, and how Christian and Catholic, goals mesh. We need to acknowledge that people of different faiths, or of no particular faith, are not on our faculties, in administrative offices, or on boards of trustees, on sufferance. We also need to make it clear that we support academic freedom, even as we insist that the diverse members of the community respect the traditions, rituals, and teachings of the Catholic faith.

A next step is to acquaint, or reacquaint, ourselves, sponsors, trustees, administrators, and faculties, with the literature on Catholic higher education. Such a review will reveal not only a rich history and tradition, but also an ethos of Catholic higher education. Such study means enmeshing ourselves, to the extent that we can, in Catholic doctrine and teaching. We do this not because the end goal is to voice our agreement with it, but to profess our respect for it. We realize that the day-to-day work in our offices, classrooms, and committee rooms does not easily lend itself to leisurely reflection on academic and administrative matters, much less to reflection on the enterprise we are trying to revitalize. Nonetheless, such study and reflection is crucial to the survival of Catholic higher education and to those who sponsor, govern, administer, or oversee it. We need, therefore, to make time to look back on the road we have traveled; to assess our present position; and to swap stories about possible futures.

These conversations and processes—including ongoing discussions about what Catholic identity means in various parts of the institution—are fundamental to academic life in general. They are especially critical for those who teach in Catholic colleges and universities where the mission is to direct a search for truth that ultimately leads to God.

CRITIQUING THE CURRICULUM

Ideally, the curricula offered at Catholic colleges and universities will further students' abilities to link knowledge, critical thinking, responsibility and the search for a God who is Truth and Love. This involves not only serious study in all disciplines but also one that is informed by faith. The link between faith and learning can be facilitated through a grounding in the liberal arts and in the development of the skills related to critical thinking. But learning in faith-based institutions of higher education cannot stop here. A curriculum must be fashioned that fosters habits of both the mind and the heart, as well as habits that support the integration of faith and learning. The curriculum must incorporate components that help students develop attitudes of reflection and contemplation, of wonder and awe, of gratitude for what we have received from God, and of a thirst for justice so that others also may know the compelling story of God's love and care for all people. To do less may be to succumb to the reductionist tendencies of our disciplines while developing an attitude of skepticism that is deadening rather than enlivening.

Developing attitudes of reflection and contemplation. Essentially, reflection and contemplation are about paying attention, and paying attention is, of course, what every academic discipline demands of us. Simone Weil, in "Reflections on the Right Use of School Studies with a View to the Love of God,"[24] argues that developing the faculty of attention forms the real object and almost sole interest of studies. Attention consists of suspending our thought and leaving it detached, but ready to receive, in its naked truth, the object that seeks entrance. Attentiveness makes us capable of looking at our suffering neighbor in a certain way and then asking, "What are you going through?"—recognizing that the sufferer exists not as a specimen from a social category, but as a person, exactly like ourselves, who was one day stamped with a special mark of affliction. "Those who are unhappy have no need for anything in this world but people capable of giving them their attention."[25] Catholic colleges and universities should graduate students who have developed the habit of reflecting and "paying attention" to the world around them and to the way they live their lives. This includes a consciousness that how they live their lives has an impact on the way others can live theirs.

Developing wonder and awe. Related to the faculty of attention is the capacity for wonder and awe. A line from a song by Heather Bishop asks, "How dare, how dare you stand there wearing all of your beauty?"[26] A contemplative is moved to say this often, gazing at a flagrantly beautiful tree; at the complex simplicity of the DNA spiral; at the brilliance of a starlit sky; at a courageous friend serenely facing death; at the intent, innocent play of a child.

This is wonder. This is awe. And wonder and awe can direct us toward truth from at least two directions: by raising questions about the way things are—a prelude to the search for truth; or by movements of the spirit that suggest a Transcendent power greater than ourselves—a prelude to the truth of God's existence. The awareness of the ability to move in both directions is a critical outcome of the type of curricula offered at Catholic colleges and universities.

Learning to thirst for justice. Contemplation, reflection, wonder, and awe quicken a sense of beauty in us. They also awaken a thirst for justice and a desire to seek it. Paolo Freire calls education "cultural action for freedom."[27] This involves a dialogue and calls for all campus actors—students, faculty, staff, and administrators—to study the human condition in order to transform it in the interest of liberation.

Freire contrasts this with "cultural action for domestication," which considers students as spectators and consumers and expects them to enter the existing social order of domination, exploitation, and consumerism without questioning or disturbing it. Might not one of the traits that helps distinguish graduates of a Catholic college or university be their willingness to "dare to disturb the universe,"[28] as T.S. Eliot put it, because of their engagement with a curriculum that educates them about global realities, poverty, injustice, and alternatives to violence as a means of solving our problems?

Developing a liberating curriculum. If we agree that engagement with the world and that the education for justice is an overarching imperative for the Catholic college or university, how will this belief be translated into the curriculum? Can we organize courses and programs around issues of social, religious, moral, and ethical concerns without having education edge into indoctrination? Can departments other than theology, religious studies, and philosophy rise to this challenge? For the Jesuit Jon Sobrino, a colleague of the El Salvador Jesuit martyrs, the danger of indoctrination is much less real than the temptation of our colleagues, administrators, boards of trustees, and congregational sponsors to tolerate various forms of injustice because of a mistaken understanding of pluralism, objectivity, rational thought, or academic freedom.

Accepting a vision like that of Sobrino implies crafting a curriculum that offers opportunities to examine human conflict from cross-cultural perspectives. It presupposes a curriculum that offers an understanding of patriarchy in its historical perspective, its variety of institutional forms, and its relation to current power relations between the sexes and among nations. It assumes a curriculum that helps students examine the relationships between race, gender, class, and ethnicity, as seen from the perspective of every discipline. It calls for a curriculum that convinces students that the human race is as capable of devising strategies for change in the realms of war and peace, ecological balance, and social justice, as it is in solving problems of disease, business management, and electronic communication.

Might then one discern the Catholic identity of a college or university in its Spirit-inspired attempts to contemplate reality, or wonder about it, both intellectually and affectively, not only from the perspective of its "incredible lightness of being", but also from the perspective of non-being, pain, poverty, oppression and death? Sobrino suggests as much in a chapter of his book, *The Principle of Mercy*. Seeing reality from its underside forces knowledge to be liberating, he says, not just descriptive. Can we develop curricula that meet this standard, perhaps in its general education and service learning requirements, that draw upon a long-standing tradition of Catholic social teaching and service to others?

Assuming that this quest for knowledge and the willingness to use it to liberate others is a worthy goal, what resources might Catholic colleges or universities commit toward this vision? Here, we suggest that a variety of resources is at their disposal because they are "institutional actors" within their local and Church communities.

CATHOLIC HIGHER EDUCATION AS INSTITUTIONAL ACTORS

All colleges and universities are institutional actors. They have highly organized structures and the power to control more resources than most individuals within a community.[29] Institutional actors, therefore, have the power to affect the economic and social well-being of their communities. This is true even of Catholic colleges and universities that are at the moment financially challenged. They, too, have the power—through the use of their presence, their ethos, their influence, and their resources—to stabilize or destabilize their communities, and to make value based statements about what is important and how we should live together through the public commitment of their resources.

Consider, for example, how Catholic colleges and universities, as major employers within a community, affect the social and economic well-being of the people whose livelihoods depend on working on or around the campus. Further consider how a decision to close a college, or even to sell or develop part of it, generates concern among the local residents who fear that such decisions will adversely affect the quality of life of the community.

Simply by existing, Catholic colleges and universities demonstrate a commitment to their local communities and provide a stabilizing influence. They suggest to current or prospective residents that the community has a future worth investing in. Thus, because institutional actors cannot easily run away, they help shape the daily decisions of individual residents and business people, decisions that ultimately affect the quality of life of the entire community.

As a locus of highly trained personnel and financial resources, institutional actors also have the capacity to bring their resources and expertise to bear on community problems. Often underestimated, the ability of Catholic colleges and universities to effect community change comes with an institutional presence and strength that eludes the individual or collective interests of those whose intentions are either self-serving or not focused on the common good. Operating out of a strong sense of service—not only to higher education but also to the community—Catholic colleges and universities have the ability to provide many pro bono or below-cost services to local civic, social, and political organizations.

As institutional actors then, Catholic colleges and universities have great potential, often unrealized, to effect change. But such is true for any institution of higher education. What roles might institutional actors that are *Catholic* colleges and universities assume within their communities? How might these institutions project our Catholic tradition, ethos, and identity? We suggest there are two possibilities.

First, a Catholic college or university could seek to become a "community of character," as Stanley Hauerwas describes it.[30] Catholic colleges and universities would then be recognized as places where people could come to hear the "story of God" found in Scripture. They would become places that implement curricula and organizational strategies that are "faithful to that story." In so doing, our colleges and universities can become hospitable communities of virtue, communities open to new people, new ideas, and new ways of thinking, even as they study Catholic religious teachings and texts. Developing such communities "may involve nothing more or less than the Christian community's willingness to provide hospitality for the stranger—particularly when the stranger so often comes in the form of our own children."[31] Such communities would not "be characterized by oppressive uniformity but by a truthfulness and a diversity of spirits that constitute the church."[32]

Secondly, Catholic colleges and universities could place their organizational skills and institutional resources (influence, money, people) at the service of the poor and the marginalized. Further, without compromising academic freedom, or even threatening their tax-exempt status, Catholic colleges and universities could, with their fiscal resources, adopt pricing and investment strategies that address unjust structures, practices, and violations of freedom and fundamental human rights.

These are but two roles that Catholic colleges and universities can play as institutional actors within their communities. What might their role be as institutional actors within the Catholic Church?

Our institutions of higher education are precisely that—institutional agents of education. As such, their primary mission remains one of teaching, research, and service that is informed, wherever possible, by faith perspectives or theological insight. Thus, while these institutions engage in or support other Church-related activities, they are not the Church's *primary* vehicle for evangelization. Nor is their mission to provide the Church's primary source of sacramental life or worship. Rather, Catholic colleges and universities could direct their resources and influence to promote the type "dialogue and inquiry" that witness "to an authentically Christian life,"[33] much as Stephen Bevans and Eleanor Doidge describe as processes appropriate to theological reflection. This effort would be especially important in a global and technological society where power structures and technological advances subsume, more often than promote, the message of the Gospel.

The thought of Bevans and Doidge gives further content to a framework for thinking about the role of Catholic colleges and universities as institutional actors. For example, by offering opportunities for "prayer, liturgy, and contemplation,"Catholic colleges and universities can help create communities of reflection and prayer, infusing their students and the local with the gifts and the courage that make it possible to act morally and responsibly. Further, through a philosophical and visible commitment to "peace, justice, and the integrity of creation," Catholic colleges and universities can become institutional actors that model direct service to the marginalized and to the poor. They can both educate and advocate for systemic change with respect to issues of race, age, violence, culture, class, and gender.

As institutional actors whose mission supports that of the Church, Catholic colleges and universities can offer opportunities for interreligious, interethnic, and intercultural dialogue. Rather than diluting Catholic identity, such opportunities will nurture it because it will arise from and reflect an attitude of respect for others and a willingness to share with and to learn from them. Such dialogue is itself, the work of justice and peacemaking, of reconciliation, forgiveness, and the healing of broken relationships.[34]

Playing the role of an institutional actor whose primary mission is teaching and learning, but which is nevertheless an agent of the Church, will require more than a commitment to a general social ethic or morality. Arriving at a common understanding of the role that colleges and universities can play as institutional actors within the Church and within communities will require a conscious and conscientious look outward that aligns these institutions with all those concerned with social justice and with the complex ethical issues posed by political, economic, social, and religious systems. It will entail a critical and value-based examination of the effects of new technologies. It will require new understandings of war and peace. It will mean a reconsideration of the often-expedient categorizations of "enemies" and "friends." It will demand more sophisticated analyses to replace the convenient and simplistic conceptualizations of who or what is good or evil. It will require attention to the precarious state of our ecological balance and the increasingly unequal distribution of resources. Finally, it will demand a commitment to nonviolent and multilateral ways to solve the domestic, national, and international problems that characterize our society.

Our willingness to engage these issues openly and honestly and, where possible, to put our institutional resources in support of our beliefs, will forcefully proclaim the Catholic identity of our colleges and universities. We will thereby creatively and effectively address John Paul's challenge in *Ex Corde Eccelsiae.*

All of this suggests that authentically Catholic colleges and universities will nourish faith and foster moral probity and a hunger and thirst for justice. They will support campus ministry and will offer a solid theological formation in an atmosphere conducive as much to reflection and contemplation, to wonder and awe, to prayer and worship as much as to critical thinking. They will be hospitable, welcoming communities that share resources with the poor, the marginalized, and the stranger.

None of this implies that those involved in Catholic higher education should distort subject matter or constrain debate to make it fit some preordained religious or moral framework. We do not have to subordinate what we do in our teaching, research, or service to some religious purpose.

We can, nevertheless, teach in such a way that the material of our disciplines opens out onto theological and spiritual realities, and to the rich realm of Catholic social teaching. We can, in our research and scholarship, tackle important moral and social questions. We can raise our students' consciousness of the interrelatedness of all of creation , and of the unity and peace that can be found in the One who is the center of our existence. We can awaken our students to the dimension of life that dips below the surface of things. In brief, Catholic colleges and universities will demonstrate their Catholic identity in an institutional ethos where teachers, administrators, staff members, trustees, and sponsors collaborate with each other and with their local communities to teach our students to "act justly, to love tenderly, and to walk humbly with our God."

NOTES

1. Peter Drucker, *Management: Tasks, Responsibilities, and Practices*, San Francisco: HarperCollins, Publishers, 1973.

2. Peter Drucker, *Managing the Non-Profit Organization: Practices and Principles*, San Francisco: HarperCollins, Publishers, 1990, p. 4.

3. Robert H.Terry, *Authentic Leadership: Courage in Action*, San Francisco: Jossey-Bass Publishers, 1993, passim.

4. For an example of how one healthcare system uses mission in its hiring practices, see Peter Giammalvo and George Longstreet, Building Leadership that Endures," *Health Progress*, May-June, 2002, pp. 50, 53, 64.

5. Many colleges have posted their actual experiences with developing mission-centered hiring practices, the policies themselves, or the results of focus groups.

6. James Heft and F. Pestello. "Hiring Practices in Catholic Colleges and Universities, *Current Issues in Catholic Higher Education*, 20 (1), pp. 89-98.

7. Daniel Goleman, *Primal Leadership: Realizing the Power of Emotional Intelligence*, Boston: Harvard Business School Press, 2002, pp. 225-248.

8. James C. Collins and Jerry I. Porras, "Building Your Companies Vision," *Harvard Business Review*, September-October 1996, p. 67.

9. Mary Kathryn Grant, "Mission-Based Planning," *Healthcare Forum Journal*, January/February 1990, pp. 15-19. See also, Amy Hollis Smessaert, "Advancing Mission in the Market Place," *Health Progress*, October 1992, pp. 38-41.

10. Personal interview with S. Judith Murphy, OSB, first principal and architect of the curriculum for Cristo Rey, May 10, 2002.

11. James D. Whitehead and Evelyn Eaton Whitehead, *Method in Ministry: Theological Reflection and Christian Ministry*, revised edition, Franklin, WI: Sheed and Ward, 1999.

12. T.S. Eliot, " The Four Quartets," in *The Complete Poems and Plays, 1909-1950*, (London: Harcourt Brace Jonavich, 1971), p. 119.

13 . Avery Dulles, *Models of the Church* (New York: Doubleday, 1978), p. 23.

14. J. Bryan Hehir, "Identity and Institutions" *Health Progress*, Nov.-Dec. 1995, p. 18.

15. Philip Selznick, *The Moral Commonwealth*, (Berkeley: University of California Press, 1992), p. 244.

16. Dulles, pp. 76-102.

17. Avery Dulles, "Narrowing the Gap," *Origins*, March 17,1994 (Vol. 23:39), p. 679.

18. John Paul II, Discourse to the "Institut Catholique de Paris," June 1, 1980: *Insegnamenti di Giovanni Paolo II*, Vol. III/1 (1980), p. 1581, as cited in John Paul II, *"Ex Corde Ecclesiae: Apostolic Constitution of the Supreme Pontiff John Paul II on Catholic Universities*, p. 1, (hereafter, *Ex Corde).*

19. Elizabeth Linehan, RSM, a presentation on "Ethics in the Academy: Academic Freedom and Academic Responsibility in a Catholic University," Saint Xavier University, Chicago: October 7, 2003.

20. *Ex Corde,* p. 2.

21. Ibid., p. 3.

22. *Ex Corde,* p. 21, citing Vatican Council II, "Declaration on Religious Liberty *Dignitatis Humanae*," n. 2: *AAS* 58 (1966), pp. 930-931.

23. David J. O'Brien, "A Collegiate Conversation," *America*, September 11, 1993, p. 19.

24. Simone Weil, in "Reflections on the Right Use of School Studies with a View to the Love of God," *The Simone Weil Reader*, edited by George A. Panichas, N.Y.: David McKay Company, Inc., 1977, pp. 44-52.

25. Ibid., p. 51.

26. Heather Bishop, "Please Me" in the album *I Love Women Who Laugh.*

27. Paolo Friere, *Cultural Action for Freedom,* Penguin Press, Harmondsworth, Middlesex, UK, 1972.

28. T. S.Eliot, "The Love Song of J. Alfred Prufrock," lines 45-46.

29. See Richard Taub's *Paths of Neighborhood Change*, University of Chicago Press: Chicago, 1984, for a broad discussion of the role of institutional actors within communities.

30. Stanley Hauerwas, *A Community of Character: Toward a Constructive Christian Social Ethic,* South Bend: University of Notre Dame Press, 1994.

31. Ibid., p. 2.

32. Ibid.

33. Stephen Bevans and Eleanor Doidge, "Theological Reflection," from *Reflection and Dialogue: What Mission Confronts Religious Life Today?"*, an unpublished monograph. Both authors are professors at Catholic Theological Union in Chicago.

34. Ibid.

Authors

MARY KATHRYN GRANT, PhD, is executive director of the Conference for Mercy Higher Education, a network of the 18 colleges and universities of the Sisters of Mercy of the Americas. Kate had previously served as executive vice president of Sponsorship and Mission Services for Holy Cross Health System Corporation (HCHSC), South Bend, Indiana; principal at Consolidated Catholic Health Care, Westchester, Illinois; director of Sponsorship for Catholic Health Association, St. Louis; and executive director of Mercy Health Conference, Farmington Hills, Michigan.

She is a prolific author and international conference and seminar speaker on a wide range of topics, particularly in the areas of mission and sponsorship, workplace spirituality, and culture formation. She is listed in *Who's Who of American Women*, 1983 and 1990, and *Who's Who of American Authors*, 1980. In 1999, she co-authored with Sister Patricia Vandenberg, CSC, then president/CEO of Holy Cross Health System, the book *After We're Gone: Creating Sustainable Sponsorship.*

PATRICIA VANDENBERG, CSC, MHA, serves as Eastern Area Coordinator for the Congregation of the Sisters of the Holy Cross. Prior to this ministry, she was president and chief executive officer of the Holy Cross Health System from 1989-2000, at the time one of the nation's largest Catholic health systems. After leading the system into a merger, she became director of the Healthcare Executive MBA at Baldwin Wallace College, Berea, Ohio.

Sister Patricia is currently a member of the CARES Commission, an advisory group of the Department of Veterans Affairs (VA) that evaluates VA healthcare services throughout the United States. A nurse by profession, she has held various clinical and administrative positions.

Her published works include a broad range of topics such as governance, spirituality at work, mission fulfillment, sponsorship, and women's spirituality.

Contributors

Kaye Ashe, OP, PhD taught and administered at Dominican University in River Forest, IL from 1969-1986. From 1986 until 1994, she served as Prioress of the Sinsinawa Dominicans. She is currently living in Berkeley and teaching at St. Mary's College in Moraga.

Kaye has contributed chapters to publications such as *Tomorrow's Church: What's Ahead for American Catholics?*, *Midwives of the Future: American Sisters Tell Their Story*, and *Candida Lund's God and Me*. She is the author of *Today's Woman, Tomorrow's Church* (1983) and *The Feminization of the Church* (1997).

Kaye has taught and lectured frequently on women's issues and has a particular interest in women's spirituality.

John A. Gallagher, PhD, is corporate director of Ethics for Catholic Healthcare Partners (CHP). As a member of the Department of Mission and Values Integration he shares responsibility for the development and implementation of systemwide strategies for integrating the mission and values throughout the organization, including its policies, practices and culture. He provides on-going assistance to the leadership of CHP in identifying emerging issues in moral theology, ethics and social justice as they impact the ministry and recommends appropriate responses.

Prior to serving CHP, he was director of Corporate Integrity at St. Joseph's Health System in Atlanta, Georgia; vice president of System Organizational Integrity and System Ethics at Holy Cross Health System, South Bend, Indiana. He was on the theological faculty of Mercy College (Detroit) and Loyola University of Chicago. He holds a doctoral degree from the Divinity School of the University of Chicago.

Dr. Gallagher has published a wide range of articles on issues of healthcare ethics. He has spoken to a variety of audiences on issues in contemporary healthcare and the theological underpinning of the Catholic healthcare ministry.

SUSAN M. SANDERS, RSM, PhD, is director of the Center for Religion and Public Discourse, associate professor of History and Political Science, and associate professor in the Graham School of Management at Saint Xavier University.

Sister Susan began her teaching career at Mother McAuley Liberal Arts High School, Chicago, and prior to coming to Saint Xavier University, taught at the University of California, Berkeley; the University of Chicago; and DePaul University, where she was Associate Professor of Public Services between 1990 and 2001. She currently serves as a member of the President's Cabinet at Saint Xavier University and as the University's administrative representative to the Lilly Fellows Program.

Sister Susan's published works includes articles in both academic and trade journals and books on non-profit healthcare. Her latest book, *Teen Dating Violence: The Invisible Peril* (2003), was released by Peter Lang Publishing.

Acknowledgements

We would like to acknowledge the users of *After We're Gone: Creating Sustainable Sponsorship* for their overwhelming response to the publication and their persistent request that we continue to share reflections and learnings from our work in sponsorship and mission.

We especially want to acknowledge and thank the following persons:

- HELEN MONKIVITICH, whose sharing of insights and experiences, as well as probing questions have help shaped our thinking

- MARY ROCH ROCKLAGE, whose companionship along the way has enriched our lives and helped to sharpen our focus

- MARYLOUISE FENNELL, whose encouragement and depth of experience expanded the context and content of this work

- MARGARET CROWLEY, whose constant pursuit of new ways of thinking inspires daringly new ways of looking at so many thinks, sponsorhip included

- And our editors, KATHE BRUNTON and CELINE ARVISU-QUINIO for their tireless work to bring this to press

To order copies of *Partners in the Between Time: Creating Sponsorship Capacity,* please contact
BookMasters, Inc.
P.O. Box 388
Ashland, OH 44805
Phone: 800.247.6553
Fax: 419.281.6883
e-mail: order@bookmasters.com

1-4 copies: $15.00 each
5 or more copies: $12.00 each
plus shipping and handling